W9-AOS-600

Pamela Geermann

chatelaine
Wonder Foods

100 easy recipes for nutritional power foods

Monda Rosenberg

Prentice
Hall
Canada

A Pearson Company
Toronto

A SMITH SHERMAN BOOK
produced in conjunction with CHATELAINE®
and published by PRENTICE HALL CANADA

Canadian Cataloguing in Publication Data

Rosenberg, Monda
    Chatelaine wonder foods : 100 easy recipes for nutritional power foods

Includes index.
ISBN 0-13-093251-5

1. Cookery. I. Title. II. Title: Wonder foods.

TX714.R664 2001   641.5'63   C00-933204-9

© 2001 Rogers Media Limited and Smith Sherman Books Inc.

All rights reserved. This publication is protected by copyright, and permission should be obtained from the publisher prior to any prohibited reproduction, storage in a retrieval system, or transmission in any form or by any means, electronic, mechanical, photocopying, recording, or likewise. For information regarding permission, write to the Permissions Department.

ISBN 0-13-093251-5

Design and page composition: PageWave Graphics Inc.

Photographs: Michael Cohn (opposite pages 48, 112, 144); Michael Mahovlich (opposite page 49); Ed O'Neil (front cover, opposite pages 16, 17, 33, 64, 80, 81, 113, 128, 129, 145); Andreas Trauttmansdorff (opposite pages 32, 65).

Colour separations: Colour Technologies

Printing: Kromar Printing

1 2 3 4 5 KR 05 04 03 02 01

Printed and bound in Canada

Cover photo: Magnificent Mango Salad
(see recipe, page 68)

Visit the Pearson PTR Canada Web site!
Send us your comments, browse our catalogues, and more. **www.pearsonptr.ca**

For recipes, health information and much more, visit the Chatelaine Web site at **www.chatelaine.com**

chatelaine

Prentice
Hall
Canada

A Pearson Company

A SMITH SHERMAN BOOK

Contents

Recipe for a Long Life

Eat well and you'll live well. Common wisdom, yes, but in the past decade science has vastly increased our understanding of exactly how to do it. An explosion of studies has shown that the right foods and therapeutic doses of some supplements offer a one-two punch in the fight against women's most common illnesses, including heart disease, cancer and osteoporosis. Although factors such as genetics and aging are beyond our control, some experts now believe you can even the odds with what you feed your body.

We've identified the top 10 beneficial foods (plus a special chapter on chocolate and its benefits) that have withstood scientific scrutiny, but more important — the test of time. *Wonder Foods* presents more than 100 recipes from these groups. Here are the foods that will give your body what it needs to have the best chance to prevent disease and promote good health. And here also is the latest news from *Chatelaine*'s Health Pages on food and how it affects you.

Defining the Terms

Are you baffled by all the scientific lingo that's now out there to describe just plain old food? Well, you're not alone. But as researchers home in on what each nutrient does, we're getting closer to finding out exactly how each one works to prevent disease. Here's a guide to the most bandied-about terms to help you sort it all out.

The Enemy

Free Radicals

No, these are not terrorists who have been released from jail. These are unstable oxygen molecules that are manufactured when your body goes through its daily digestive paces. But free radicals can act like terrorists when they invade your body after exposure to a high-fat diet, environmental pollution and tobacco smoke. These highly reactive molecules can damage healthy cell membranes and tissue, which have been implicated in cancer, heart disease, Alzheimer's and many other conditions.

The Warriors

Antioxidants

These are the good guys, the anti-terrorists who fight free radicals. Good sources include a rainbow of fresh fruit and veggies, as well as green and black teas.

Bioflavonoids

Sound like something half human and half robot? Nope. Bioflavonoids are antioxidants that support the work vitamin C does. They are found in the white spongy coating of citrus fruit peels and sections, leafy veggies, red onions and, yes, even coffee. Recently, bioflavonoids have been found to lower cholesterol.

Beta Carotene

As you might guess from its name, carrots are one abundant source of this powerful antioxidant. Once you eat anything with an orange or red hue, such as carrots, squash, sweet potatoes, cantaloupe, pink grapefruit and tomatoes, the beta carotene is converted into vitamin A, which is essential for cell growth and development. Dark green leafy veggies have beta carotene in them, too.

Phyto Helpers

Isoflavones

These are plant compounds called phytoestrogens that mimic female hormones. On the one hand, they provide estrogen-like compounds when estrogen is low, and on the other, they block estrogen receptors in breast tissue, providing some protective effect against breast cancer. Soybeans, tofu and soy milk, chickpeas, kidney beans and lentils are good sources of isoflavones.

Lignans

These are nutrient compounds found in flaxseed, walnuts and canola oil. Lignans are another kind of phytoestrogen that act like a weak form of estrogen in the body.

Organic or Not

When we think of organic food, many of us share some foggy idea of pesticide-free produce that is hard to find and costs a small fortune. But organic food is not a fringe fad. It is a growing industry that continues to climb every year. And it's not just relegated to health stores, but is sweeping grocery chains such as Loblaws and Dominion across the country.

Organic farms have a strict set of standards dictated by the Organic Crop Producers and Processors of Canada. To be certified organic means that the farmers must follow a whole slew of guidelines including no chemical pesticides, no polluting chemical fertilizers, no fertilizer that contains human, animal or industrial waste, no drugs given to livestock such as antibiotics, hormones and growth promoters and no genetically modified organisms.

If you're interested in exploring organic foods for yourself and your family, there are many services that now deliver organic food directly to your door or neighbourhood. Or to find a list of organic farmers' markets across Canada, visit: www.inforganics.com/Food/navigation/farmers_markets.htm.

Fats: The Good, the Bad and the Ugly

Fats are the enemy, right? If only it were that simple. Fact is, some fats are your body's allies. Here's how to tell friend from foe:

The Good

Monounsaturated fats help prevent coronary heart disease by lowering bad cholesterol levels. These good fats may also help prevent colon cancer. So, where can you find them? Olive, canola and peanut oils, avocados and nuts.

Polyunsaturated fats, or omega-3 fatty acids, are also great for your heart and are terrific breast cancer fighters. Omega-3s can lower the levels of triglycerides and make platelets less likely to form blood clots, reducing your risk of heart attack and strokes. And, when omega-3 fatty acids accumulate in the breast, they weaken the estrogen signal. Best sources: fatty fish such as salmon, tuna, sardines, mackerel and herring; plant sources include flaxseed and walnuts.

The Bad

Hydrogenated fats are liquid vegetable oils that have had hydrogen atoms injected into them so that they can be used for such items as margarine. The chemical process makes these oils become saturated (see The Ugly) as well as creating another kind of fat called trans-fatty acids, which actually increase levels of bad cholesterol (LDL) and suppress the good cholesterol (HDL). Choose margarine that is non-hydrogenated or read nutrition labels for saturated fat levels. And avoid fried and fast foods and commercially made snack items such as cookies, pastries, potato chips and doughnuts.

The Ugly

Saturated fats in animal products such as butter, cheese and meat are what make cholesterol levels rise. Choose lean cuts of meat and limit servings to three times a week; buy low-fat cheese and milk.

Eggs and Cholesterol

Contrary to what you may believe, eggs, which have a high cholesterol content, do not cause your blood cholesterol levels to rise very much. Confusing? This is the way it works: your body makes about 70 percent of the cholesterol circulating in your body from saturated and trans-fatty acids found in foods such as meat and hydrogenated margarine. Most of the cholesterol from eggs gets digested and eliminated. Bottom line: it's okay to eat eggs but, as with anything, in moderation. People with high cholesterol levels should limit their intake to two eggs a week.

The Numbers Explained

Wonder Foods provides you with must-have information for each recipe on calorie, total fat (including saturated and cholesterol) and carbohydrate content, as well as the amount of protein, iron, calcium, sodium and fibre. In addition, we also indicate when a recipe is an excellent or good source of a particular vitamin, mineral or dietary fibre. The nutrient analysis was produced by Info Access (1988) Inc., Toronto, Ontario, using the Nutritional Accounting component of the CBORD Menu Management System. Here's some other info to keep in mind:

- Optional ingredients and ingredients called for in unspecified amounts are omitted from our analysis.

- We analyse the imperial ingredient amounts only.

- When there's a choice of ingredients (for example, tofu or chicken), the first ingredient is the one analysed. And when a quantity range for ingredients is given, the smallest quantity is the one analysed. As well, an analysis is based on the larger number of servings when there is a range.

The following criteria have been used to evaluate the recipe servings as excellent or good sources:

Vitamins and Minerals
The Guide to Food Labelling and Advertising, March 1996, and amendments (Canadian Food Inspection Agency) states that a serving of food which supplies 15 percent of the Recommended Daily Intake (RDI) for a vitamin or mineral (30 percent for vitamin C) may be described as a "good source of" or "high" in a nutrient; and if it supplies 25 percent of the RDI (50 percent for vitamin C), it may be described as an "excellent source of" or "very high source of" that nutrient.

Dietary Fibre
The Guide states that a food providing at least 2 grams per serving may be described as a "source" or as containing a "moderate" amount of dietary fibre; a food providing at least 4 grams may be described as containing "high" amounts and one providing at least 6 grams as containing "very high" amounts.

Daily Nutrient Intake for Women

19 to 49 years	50 to 74 years
1,900 calories	1,800 calories
51 g protein	54 g protein
1,000 mg calcium*	1,500 mg calcium*
13 mg iron	8 mg iron

*Recommendation from the Osteoporosis Society of Canada

Recipe Index by Nutrient
Need more folic acid or calcium in your diet? See our handy guide on page 156.

antioxidants

vitamin C

selenium

Brassica

folic acid

Brassica vegetables, also known as cruciferous vegetables, are rich in antioxidants and phytochemicals (see page 66). Studies show that people who eat a lot of these vegetables have a reduced risk of disease. Broccoli, cabbage, kale, cauliflower, mustard greens and turnips are high in the phytochemicals dithiolthiones and isothiocyanates that are thought to deter hormone-related diseases such as breast and prostate cancer. Most also come with a healthy amount of folic acid, fibre, selenium and vitamin C.

phytochemicals

Curried Cauliflower Bisque

Turn half a cauliflower into this appetite-soothing low-cal soup. It's great hot or cold served with olive focaccia bread.

10-oz	can condensed chicken broth	284-mL
½ to 1 tsp	curry paste or 2 tsp (10 mL) curry powder	2 to 5 mL
½ tsp	ground cumin	2 mL
½	head cauliflower florets, about 4 cups (1 L)	½
½ cup	light sour cream	125 mL
2	green onions, thinly sliced	2
¼ cup	finely chopped fresh coriander (optional)	50 mL

1. In a large saucepan, combine condensed soup, curry paste or powder, cumin and cauliflower. Cover and bring to a boil over high heat, stirring occasionally. Reduce heat to low and boil gently, partially covered and stirring often, until cauliflower is soft, from 15 to 20 minutes.

2. Then whirl soup in a food processor or blender until puréed. Return to saucepan. Whisk in sour cream. Thin, if necessary, with milk or water. Heat on low, stirring occasionally, just until hot. Serve sprinkled with green onions and/or coriander. Soup will keep well, tightly covered in the refrigerator, for up to 2 days or can be frozen.

MAKES: 4 cups (1 L)
PREPARATION TIME: 10 minutes / COOKING TIME: 25 minutes

Nutrients per cup (250 mL): 7.2 g protein, 2.8 g total fat (1.2 g saturated, 5 mg cholesterol) 8.5 g carbohydrates, 0.9 mg iron, 93 mg calcium, 506 mg sodium, 1.8 g fibre, 85 calories

Excellent source of vitamin C.
Good source of niacin and folic acid.

Puréed Broccoli-Carrot Soup

Expect requests for seconds of this satisfying soup that's thick with "little bites" of fresh vegetables. This soup is made with an unusual cooking technique — the vegetables are almost puréed before cooking. Serve with thick slices of whole wheat bread.

1	large or 2 small heads of broccoli	1
4	carrots	4
2	stalks celery	2
4	small onions	4
4 tbsp	butter	60 mL
6 cups	chicken broth or bouillon	1.5 L
¼ tsp	each of dried basil, leaf thyme and oregano	1 mL
½ tsp	salt	2 mL
¼ cup	all-purpose flour	50 mL
2 cups	homogenized milk or half & half cream (optional)	500 mL

1. Cut florets from broccoli. Peel broccoli stems and carrots. Cut stems, carrots and celery into 1-inch (2.5-cm) pieces. Add half of vegetables to food processor. Pulse until coarsely ground to about the size of sesame seeds. Repeat with remaining vegetables. Set aside while continuing with recipe.

2. Cut onions in half. Whirl in food processor until coarsely ground. In a large saucepan, heat 1 tablespoon (15 mL) butter over medium heat. Add onions and sauté, stirring often until soft, 5 minutes.

3. Add all the vegetables. Cook, stirring often over medium heat until vegetables are slighted softened, 5 minutes. Then stir in chicken broth, seasonings and salt. Increase heat to high and bring to a boil, stirring occasionally. Reduce heat to low, partially cover and simmer for 20 minutes to soften vegetables.

4. To thicken soup, melt remaining 3 tablespoons (45 mL) butter in a small dish in microwave or in a small saucepan over low heat. Stir in flour until smooth. When vegetables are done as you like, increase heat to medium. When bubbling intensely, stir constantly and slowly whisk in flour-butter mixture. Stir often until thickened, about 5 minutes. Taste and stir in milk or cream, if you like. Heat just until hot. Do not boil. Soup will keep well, tightly covered in the refrigerator, for up to 2 days. If you are going to freeze soup, it's best to add milk or cream after reheating.

MAKES: 9 cups (2.25 L)

PREPARATION TIME: 20 minutes / COOKING TIME: 30 minutes

Nutrients per cup (250 mL): 6.4 g protein, 6.4 g total fat (3.5 g saturated, 14 mg cholesterol) 13.0 g carbohydrates, 1.4 mg iron, 58 mg calcium, 744 mg sodium, 3.1 g fibre, 130 calories

Excellent source of vitamins A and C.
Good source of niacin and folic acid.
Moderate amount of dietary fibre.

Apple-Scented Curried Cauliflower

Cauliflower, like its cousin broccoli, is high in vitamin C and a good source of potassium.
Enjoy it as a side dish or main event, as in this delightful colourful curry with tomatoes and peas.

1	large cauliflower	1
3	potatoes, peeled (optional)	3
1 tbsp	olive or vegetable oil	15 mL
1	regular or red onion, chopped	1
2	minced garlic cloves	2
2 tbsp	curry powder	30 mL
2 tsp	cumin powder	10 mL
2 tbsp	all-purpose flour	30 mL
2 cups	apple juice, water or chicken broth	500 mL
2	large ripe tomatoes, unpeeled	2
1 cup	frozen peas	250 mL
½ tsp	salt	2 mL
2 tbsp	freshly squeezed lemon juice	30 mL

1. Cut cauliflower into bite-size pieces. If using, cut potatoes into 1-inch (2.5-cm) cubes. They should each measure about 4 cups (1 L). Set aside. Heat oil in a large saucepan over medium heat. Stir in chopped onion and garlic. Sprinkle with curry powder and cumin. Stir often until onion just begins to soften, from 2 to 3 minutes.

2. Stirring constantly, sprinkle with flour. Continue stirring until flour is evenly absorbed. Stir in apple juice, water or chicken broth. (Apple juice adds a pleasant natural sweetness.) Continue cooking, stirring often, until mixture begins to thicken, about 2 minutes. Stir in cauliflower and potatoes. Cover and bring to a boil. Then reduce heat to low and simmer, stirring often.

3. Meanwhile, cut tomatoes into large chunks. After curry has simmered about 15 minutes and potatoes are almost tender, stir in tomatoes, peas, salt and lemon juice. Continue simmering, stirring often, until peas are hot, from 3 to 5 more minutes. Serve with roasted chicken or grilled fish or as a vegetarian main course with steamed rice and a cucumber raita.

MAKES: 7 cups (1.75 L)
PREPARATION TIME: 15 minutes / COOKING TIME: 25 minutes

Nutrients per cup (250 mL): 4.1 g protein, 2.8 g total fat (0.3 g saturated, 0 mg cholesterol), 22.7 g carbohydrates, 2.3 mg iron, 58 mg calcium, 194 mg sodium, 3.9 g fibre, 122 calories

Excellent source of vitamin C and folic acid.
Good source of vitamin B6 and iron.
Moderate amount of dietary fibre.

Spiced Brussels Sprouts

Brussels sprouts, so named because they were first grown in — where else — Brussels, are a member of the cabbage family. Like other members of this family, sprouts are linked with lower rates of cancer and can help prevent heart disease. These sprouts can be prepared ahead and are a must on many Christmas menus.

2 lbs	Brussels sprouts	1 kg
2	small or 1 large red onion or cooking onion	2
3 tbsp	butter	45 mL
1 tsp	celery seed	5 mL
2 tsp	ground cumin	10 mL
¼ tsp	hot red chili flakes	1 mL
½ tsp	salt	2 mL

1. Rinse sprouts. Trim stems. Remove loose outer leaves. Cut a small "x" in bottom of each. Bring a large saucepan of water to a boil. Add sprouts and boil gently, uncovered, just until a fork can be inserted in base without a lot of resistance, from 6 minutes for small sprouts to 12 minutes for large sprouts. Immediately drain and rinse with cold water to stop cooking. When chilled, drain well. If making ahead, store in the refrigerator in a resealable plastic bag for up to 2 days.

2. When ready to serve, peel onions, slice in half, then thinly slice. Melt butter in a large deep frying pan. Add onions, seasonings and salt. Stir often over medium heat, from 5 to 8 minutes, to sweeten onions. Then add sprouts. Cover and stir often until hot, from 8 to 10 minutes.

MAKES: 8 servings

PREPARATION TIME: 15 minutes / COOKING TIME: 19 minutes

Nutrients per serving: 3.6 g protein, 5.2 g total fat (2.8 g saturated, 12 mg cholesterol), 14.4 g carbohydrates, 1.9 mg iron, 61 mg calcium, 213 mg sodium, 5.6 g fibre, 104 calories

Excellent source of vitamin C and folic acid.
High amount of dietary fibre.

Glazed Sprouts and Onions

This great make-ahead side dish is packed with Brussels sprouts, which are especially rich in folic acid and a good source of fibre and vitamin C. And a whole cup of cooked sprouts rings in at a mere 50 calories.

8 cups	small Brussels sprouts, 1¾ lbs (875 g)	2 L
1	large red onion, peeled	1
1 tbsp	butter	15 mL
1 cup	chicken broth	250 mL
2 tbsp	granulated sugar	30 mL
2 tbsp	white vinegar	30 mL
½ tsp	ground black pepper	2 mL
¼ tsp	salt (optional)	1 mL
2 to 4 tbsp	chopped fresh dill	30 to 50 mL

1. Rinse sprouts. Trim stems. Remove loose outer leaves. Cut a small "x" in bottom of each. Halve any sprouts larger than a walnut. If making ahead, store in the refrigerator in a resealable plastic bag for up to 2 days.

2. Meanwhile, slice onion into rings. Slice rings in half. Melt butter in a large deep frying pan over medium heat. Add onions and sauté until soft, about 5 minutes. Add broth, sugar, vinegar and pepper. Bring to a boil. Add salt only if using unsalted broth. If making ahead, place mixture in a jar, seal and refrigerate.

3. To cook, combine sprouts and jar contents in a large pan over medium-high heat. Bring to a boil, then reduce heat to medium-low. Partially cover. Boil gently, stirring often, until ends of sprouts are fork-tender, from 15 to 17 minutes. Sprinkle generously with fresh dill.

MAKES: 8 servings

PREPARATION TIME: 20 minutes

MAKE-AHEAD COOKING TIME: 5 minutes / FINISHING TIME: 15 minutes

Nutrients per serving: 3.7 g protein, 2.2 g total fat (1.1 g saturated, 4 mg cholesterol), 16.2 g carbohydrates, 1.4 mg iron, 47 mg calcium, 205 mg sodium, 4.9 g fibre, 87 calories

Excellent source of vitamin C and folic acid.
High amount of dietary fibre.

Sweet-and-Sour Coleslaw

We've given an old-fashioned salad a modern spin by adding crisp snow peas and seductive coriander. Cabbage is one of the least expensive vegetables in the brassica family. One cup (250 mL) of shredded raw cabbage has just 18 calories and is fat-free. The snow peas add protein and soluble fibre, which helps lower blood cholesterol.

1	cabbage (½ green and ½ red cabbage or 1 red or green cabbage)	1
2 cups	snow peas	500 mL
1	red onion	1
¾ cup	white vinegar	175 mL
⅓ cup	granulated sugar	75 mL
¼ cup	olive oil	50 mL
½	small onion, grated	½
1 tsp	salt	5 mL
1 tsp	dry mustard	5 mL
½ tsp	celery seeds	2 mL
¼ cup	finely chopped coriander	50 mL

1. Using a large knife or food processor fitted with a slicing disc, thinly shred cabbage. It should measure about 12 cups (3 L). Slice snow peas lengthwise into thin strips. Halve red onion, place cut-side down on a cutting board, then thinly slice. Combine all in a bowl.

2. In a saucepan, bring vinegar, sugar, oil, grated onion, salt, mustard and celery seeds to a boil over medium-high heat. Stir often, until sugar is dissolved. Pour hot dressing over vegetables and stir in along with coriander until evenly coated. Immediately refrigerate. Do not cover. When chilled, cover and keep refrigerated. Stir occasionally to evenly distribute dressing. Salad can be served once it's chilled, but it's best after overnight refrigeration.

MAKES: 15 cups (3.75 L)

PREPARATION TIME: 25 minutes / COOKING TIME: 5 minutes

REFRIGERATION TIME: 45 minutes

Nutrients per ½ cup (125 mL): 0.7 g protein, 1.9 g total fat (0.3 g saturated, 0 mg cholesterol), 5.8 g carbohydrates, 0.3 mg iron, 20 mg calcium, 81 mg sodium, 0.9 g fibre, 40 calories

Good source of vitamin C.

Italian Basil and Rapini Risotto

Rapini, a trendy relative of cabbage and broccoli, adds a zesty, bold edge when paired as it is here with mild risotto. Valued for its pungent edge, rapini is also known as broccoli raab, Italian broccoli or Chinese flowering cabbage. It's a rich source of potassium and high in the antioxidant beta carotene.

1	bunch rapini	1
	or 2 cups (500 mL) chopped broccolini	
2	large ripe plum tomatoes	2
3 to 4	green onions	3 to 4
1 tbsp	butter	15 mL
2	minced garlic cloves	2
1 cup	short-grain rice, preferably Arborio	250 mL
1 cup	dry white wine	250 mL
¼ to ½ tsp	hot red chili flakes	1 to 2 mL
10-oz	can undiluted chicken broth	282-mL
1½ to 1¾ cups	water	375 to 425 mL
10	fresh large basil leaves	10
½ cup	freshly grated Parmesan cheese	125 mL

1. Clean and chop rapini. Seed and coarsely chop tomatoes. Thinly slice onions. Melt butter in a large wide saucepan over medium heat. Add garlic and sauté for 1 minute. Add rice, stirring until coated with butter, about 1 minute. Stir in wine and chili flakes. Stir gently until rice absorbs all of the wine.

2. Immediately stir in broth, ¼ cup (50 mL) at a time, stirring often and waiting until almost all liquid is absorbed before adding next ¼ cup (50 mL). Then stir in 1 cup (250 mL) water in a similar manner. This process, which will take at least 20 minutes, is necessary to achieve creaminess.

3. After 1 cup (250 mL) water has been added, stir in rapini. Continue adding water until a total of 1½ cups (375 mL) has been added. Then continue stirring until rice is tender. Add remaining ¼ cup (50 mL) water only if needed for a soupy texture. Shred basil and stir in with cheese, tomatoes and onions. Serve in soup bowls as a main course or as a side dish with grilled chicken or fish.

MAKES: 4 to 6 servings
PREPARATION TIME: 15 minutes / COOKING TIME: 30 minutes

Nutrients per serving: 7.8 g protein, 4.8 g total fat (2.9 g saturated, 12 mg cholesterol), 31 g carbohydrates, 1.1 mg iron, 205 mg calcium, 477 mg sodium, 1.6 g fibre, 208 calories

Good source of vitamin A, calcium and magnesium.

Kale and Hot Sausage Soup

Especially rich in vitamins and minerals, assertive kale is at its best in soups and stews. You're also getting calcium here, not just from the kale, but from the beans, too.

2	linguiça chorizo or hot Italian sausage	2
1 tsp	vegetable oil	5 mL
2	onions, chopped	2
3	large minced garlic cloves	3
4	large potatoes, peeled and cubed	4
2	carrots, chopped	2
28-oz	can diced or whole tomatoes, well drained, or 1 seeded, chopped sweet red pepper	796-mL
8 cups	chicken broth	2 L
1	bay leaf	1
¼ tsp	hot red chili flakes or paprika (optional)	1 mL
2 cups	shredded cabbage	500 mL
8 to 10	kale leaves, stems removed	8 to 10
2 cups	cooked navy beans	500 mL
½ tsp	salt	2 mL
¼ tsp	freshly ground black pepper	1 mL

1. Coarsely chop sausage. Heat oil in a large saucepan over medium heat. Add sausage. Sauté until lightly browned, about 7 minutes. Remove and drain on a paper towel. Pour fat from pan, leaving a film.

2. Add onions and garlic and sauté for 5 minutes. Add sausage, vegetables, drained tomatoes, broth, bay leaf and hot red chili flakes, if using. Bring to a boil, uncovered. Add cabbage. Reduce heat to low, cover and simmer for 15 minutes.

3. Meanwhile, cut kale leaves into bite-size pieces. Drain beans. When soup has simmered 15 minutes, stir in kale and beans. Simmer until kale is done as you like, up to 10 minutes. Taste and add salt and pepper, if needed. Remove bay leaf. Covered and refrigerated, soup will keep for 3 days or freeze.

MAKES: 16 cups (4 L)

PREPARATION TIME: 20 minutes / COOKING TIME: 35 minutes

Nutrients per cup (250 mL): 7.7 g protein, 4 g total fat, (1.3 g saturated, 6 mg cholesterol), 19.7 g carbohydrates, 1.5 mg iron, 47 mg calcium, 1,068 mg sodium, 3.4 g fibre, 144 calories

Excellent source of vitamin A.
Good source of niacin, vitamin B6 and folic acid.
Moderate amount of dietary fibre.

Hot Oriental Shrimp and Basil Noodles

This very easy noodle dish is great eaten hot from the pan or at room temperature. It's made here with shrimp, but you can use leftover strips of cooked chicken, beef or cubes of firm tofu.

½ lb	dried rice-vermicelli noodles or noodle threads	250 g
⅓ cup	soy sauce	75 mL
1 tsp	hot chili-garlic sauce	5 mL
1 tsp	freshly squeezed lime juice	5 mL
½ lb	small fresh or frozen shrimp, peeled	250 g
2 tbsp	vegetable oil	30 mL
1	onion, chopped	1
1 tbsp	finely minced ginger	15 mL
2	minced garlic cloves	2
8 cups	shredded napa, green or Savoy cabbage	2 L
4	green onions, sliced diagonally	4
1	carrot, coarsely shredded (optional)	1
½ cup	shredded fresh basil	125 mL
½	lime	½

1. Place noodles in a large bowl. Cover with boiling water. Stir to separate. Soak just until noodles are soft but still firm, 8 minutes. (They will cook more with sauce.) Stir soy with chili-garlic sauce and 1 teaspoon (5 mL) lime juice. If shrimp are frozen, rinse with cold water until ice crystals are melted.

2. Meanwhile, in a large wide frying pan or wok, heat oil over medium-high heat. Add onion, ginger and garlic. Stir-fry 2 minutes. Add shrimp, cabbage, green onions and carrot. Stir-fry until shrimp start to turn bright pink, about 2 minutes. Drain noodles well and add to pan along with soy sauce mixture. Toss until heated through and shrimp are bright pink, from 3 to 5 minutes. Sprinkle with basil and squeeze juice from lime over top. Taste and add more chili-garlic sauce and lime juice, if needed.

MAKES: 3 to 4 servings

PREPARATION TIME: 25 minutes / SOAKING TIME: 8 minutes

COOKING TIME: 7 minutes

Nutrients per serving: 14.3 g protein, 8.4 g total fat (0.8 g saturated, 65 mg cholesterol) 59.5 g carbohydrates, 2.3 mg iron, 166 mg calcium, 1,496 mg sodium, 4.6 g fibre, 370 calories

Excellent source of vitamins C and B6 and folic acid. **Good source of** vitamin A, calcium and iron. **High amount of** dietary fibre.

Health Wonders

Brassica All-Stars

Broccoli contains a variety of nutrients including beta carotene, which the body converts to vitamin A, essential calcium, fibre, indoles – a phytochemical (see page 66) that may help protect against breast cancer – and folic acid, a B vitamin that can help prevent birth defects such as spina bifida. It's this group effort that scientists believe may be what results in disease-fighting capabilities. Just one cup (250 mL) of raw broccoli florets has almost as much vitamin C as a glass of orange juice, but has just 13 calories.

Brussels sprouts are one fibre-rich little vegetable. These small cabbage-like buds are one of our highest fibre vegetables. One-half cup (125 mL) of cooked Brussels sprouts contains about 3.5 g. They also contain healthy amounts of vitamin A, potassium, folic acid and almost our daily supply of vitamin C. All for less than 40 calories.

Cabbage is one of the least expensive vegetables in the brassica family, which are high in fibre and contain vitamin C and other antioxidants. One cup (250 mL) of shredded raw cabbage has just 18 calories and is fat-free.

Cauliflower is high in vitamin C and potassium. It also contains a reasonable amount of protein and iron.

Preparing Produce

● Slicing and dicing into small pieces causes vitamin loss when cooked because more plant cells are exposed to water. Cut pieces uniform in size and approximately 1 inch (2.5 cm) thick.

● Cook vegetables soon after you've chopped them as some vitamins – especially C – deteriorate when exposed to oxygen.

● If you peel veggies, you lose some of the vitamins and fibre. So leave the skins on when boiling or roasting. Brush off dirt, bacteria and pesticide residues and rinse with cold water.

● Remember that vitamins C and B, as well as riboflavin and niacin, in broccoli and turnip greens dissolve in water. Save the cooking water for another dish, such as a soup base.

● Vitamins A, E and K found in cabbage and cauliflower dissolve in fat. Use just a little oil when stir-frying so there is no need to leave behind the nutrient-rich oil when serving.

Lemony Chicken Spring Fling

Toss this fresh-tasting broccoli stir-fry with sautéed new potatoes for a low-cal feast. One cup (250 mL) of raw broccoli florets has almost as much vitamin C as a glass of orange juice, but has just 13 calories.

½	lemon	½
½ cup	chicken broth or bouillon	125 mL
1 tsp	cornstarch	5 mL
2	minced garlic cloves	2
1 tsp	chopped fresh tarragon or ¼ tsp (1 mL) dried tarragon	5 mL
½ tsp	salt	2 mL
¼ tsp	freshly ground black pepper	1 mL
1	onion, peeled	1
1	small yellow pepper or yellow zucchini	1
1 lb	skinless, boneless chicken breasts, about 3 breasts	500 g
2 tbsp	vegetable oil	30 mL
1	small head broccoli or 1 bunch asparagus, about ½ lb (250 g), cut into bite-size pieces	1
⅓ cup	green peas	75 mL

1. Finely grate 2 teaspoons (10 mL) peel from lemon and squeeze out 3 tablespoons (45 mL) juice. In a small bowl, whisk 1 tablespoon (15 mL) juice and peel with broth, cornstarch, garlic, tarragon, salt and pepper. Cut onion in half, then thinly slice. Cut pepper into thin strips. Slice chicken into bite-size strips.

2. Heat oil in a large frying pan or wok over medium-high heat. Add onion and cook, stirring often, for 3 minutes. Increase heat to high and add chicken. Stir-fry until chicken takes on a golden colour, about 3 minutes. Add broccoli and stir-fry for 1 minute. Stir broth mixture and pour into pan. Add yellow pepper and peas. Stir until peas are hot, from 1 to 2 minutes. Stir in 1 tablespoon (15 mL) lemon juice. Taste and add more tarragon, salt, pepper and remaining lemon juice, if needed.

MAKES: 4 servings

PREPARATION TIME: 10 minutes / COOKING TIME: 8 minutes

Nutrients per serving: 29.6 g protein, 9.1 g total fat (1.1 g saturated, 66 mg cholesterol), 11.2 g carbohydrates, 1.5 mg iron, 52 mg calcium, 465 mg sodium, 3.3 g fibre, 244 calories

Excellent source of vitamin C and B6.
Good source of vitamin A and folic acid.

Chicken-Vegetable Biryani

Use leftover chicken or turkey to make this exotically flavoured stick-to-your-ribs dinner. And it's fast enough to whip together any night of the week.

1 tbsp	vegetable oil	15 mL
1	onion	1
1 cup	long-grain rice	250 mL
3 tbsp	biryani paste or 2 tbsp (30 mL) mild curry paste (see Tip, below)	45 mL
28-oz	can diced tomatoes, including juice	796-mL
1 cup	water	250 mL
½ tsp	salt	2 mL
2 cups	cooked chicken or turkey, cut into bite-size strips	500 mL
2 cups	mixed vegetables, such as small broccoli florets and thinly sliced carrots or frozen mixed vegetables	500 mL

1. Heat oil in a large wide saucepan over medium heat. Chop onion, then add to oil. Sauté until onion is softened, about 5 minutes. Add rice and biryani paste and stir constantly for 2 minutes. Add tomatoes, including juice, water and salt. Cover and bring to a boil.

2. Then reduce heat to low and simmer, tightly covered and without stirring, for 15 minutes. Stir in chicken and vegetables. Cover and continue simmering until water is absorbed and rice is tender, from 5 to 12 more minutes. Serve hot with Indian nan or chapati bread. Also great cold as a rice salad.

MAKES: 4 servings

PREPARATION TIME: 15 minutes / COOKING TIME: 27 minutes

TIP: Biryani and curry paste are sold in large jars and plastic tubs in the ethnic food section of many large supermarkets or in Indian grocery stores. Curry pastes vary dramatically in strength. If using regular-strength curry paste, start with 1 teaspoon (5 mL).

Nutrients per serving: 27.1 g protein, 15.8 g total fat (2.3 g saturated, 62 mg cholesterol), 52.7 g carbohydrates, 3.1 mg iron, 98 mg calcium, 1,029 mg sodium, 4.7 g fibre, 462 calories

Excellent source of vitamins A and B6.
Good source of vitamin C, folic acid and iron
High amount of dietary fibre.

magnesium

Dairy, low-fat

calcium

With one in four women destined to develop osteoporosis, we all should be loading up on calcium. We know dairy products build strong bones, but how many of us down the four glasses of milk a day needed to top up the calcium reservoir? To help you fill that gap, here are recipes brimming with taste, but using low-fat versions of milk, yogurt or sour cream. The only thing that's reduced is the fat and calories. These recipes are still overflowing with calcium, potassium and magnesium.

potassium

Cool Cucumber-Buttermilk Soup

When hot weather has you craving light drinks, don't forsake your intake of milk — an important source of calcium and vitamins A and D, essential in the prevention of osteoporosis. Most women require at least 1,000 milligrams of calcium a day. Besides drinking a glass of milk (which contains about 300 milligrams of calcium), this cold soup is a wonderful hot-weather refresher that's an easy way to boost your calcium intake.

1	English cucumber	1
4 cups	buttermilk	1 L
1 tsp	freshly squeezed lemon juice	5 mL
½ tsp	salt	2 mL
pinch	freshly ground pepper	pinch
½ cup	light sour cream (optional)	125 mL

1. Cut unpeeled cucumber into chunks. Purée in a food processor until coarsely ground. Drain pulp and discard juice. Stir pulp with remaining ingredients until well blended. You can serve right away, but soup is better when it's icy cold, so refrigerate, covered, up to 1 day.

MAKES: 6 cups (1.5 L)
PREPARATION TIME: 10 minutes

Nutrients per cup (250 mL): 6.1 g protein, 1.6 g total fat (1 g saturated, 6 mg cholesterol), 10 g carbohydrates, 0.2 mg iron, 209 mg calcium, 373 mg sodium, 0.5 g fibre, 78 calories

Good source of calcium and vitamin B_{12}.

Frozen Banana-Berry Smoothie

Satisfying smoothies are fast to whirl up and are an enjoyable way to nourish ourselves without guilt. Just choose ingredients rich in nutrients such as strawberries, an excellent source of vitamin C, and buttermilk, a great source of calcium. However, keep in mind when purchasing strawberries that some research shows they can have a high pesticide concentration. You may wish to look for organic strawberries (see page 5 for more information on organic produce). For more smoothie tips, see below.

2	large very ripe bananas, peeled and frozen	2
1	pint fresh strawberries	1
2 cups	low-fat yogurt or milk	500 mL
pinch	nutmeg	pinch

1. Cut bananas into 1-inch (2.5-cm) pieces. Cut berries in half. In a blender or food processor, blend all ingredients until smooth. For a thick milkshake texture, chill berries and place blender jar in freezer for 30 minutes before using. Add sugar, if needed.

MAKES: 4 cups (1 L)

PREPARATION TIME: 5 minutes

SMOOTHIES: A HEALTHY BLEND

Dairy products often form the base for smoothies. Blend in ingredients rich in nutrients that focus on your individual health concerns and you'll have a satisfying, nutritious drink in minutes.

- Beta carotene helps our bodies fight disease. Many orange-yellow and red fruit and vegetables are high in beta carotene. Apricots, mangoes and cantaloupe are particularly good in smoothies.
- Folic acid is especially important for women planning to get pregnant and during pregnancy as it helps prevent certain birth defects. Folic acid is also important to protect your heart. It lowers the levels of homocysteine, which is linked to an increased risk for heart disease. Adding brewer's yeast, orange juice or wheat germ to smoothies is an easy way to increase your folic acid intake.

Nutrients per cup (250 mL): 7.6 g protein, 2.5 g total fat (1.4 g saturated, 7 mg cholesterol), 30.8 g carbohydrates, 0.6 mg iron, 240 mg calcium, 86 mg sodium, 3.1 g fibre, 166 calories

Excellent source of vitamins C, B_6 and B_{12}. **Good source of** calcium and folic acid.
Moderate amount of dietary fibre.

Light Yet Creamy Celeriac Mashed Potatoes

The creaminess in these potatoes comes from low-fat buttermilk while celeriac (a celery-flavoured root vegetable) adds another taste dimension and important dietary fibre.

8	potatoes, peeled and quartered	8
1	celeriac	1
4	garlic cloves, peeled	4
pinch	salt	pinch
½ tsp	Dijon mustard	2 mL
½ tsp	salt	2 mL
¾ cup	buttermilk	175 mL
pinch	white pepper	pinch
	chives or green onions, sliced	

1. Place potatoes in a large saucepan of cold water. Place over high heat. Peel and cut celeriac into cubes. Rinse celeriac to remove any grit, then add to potatoes along with garlic and a generous pinch of salt. Add more water, if needed, to cover vegetables completely. Cover and bring to a boil. Reduce heat so water gently boils until vegetables are very tender, from 25 to 30 minutes.

2. Drain vegetables. Remove garlic to a dish. Mash with a fork and return to potatoes. Then mash potatoes and celeriac with a potato masher or food mill, or using an electric beater, beat until fluffy. Do not use a food processor. Add Dijon and ½ tsp (2 mL) salt. Gradually beat in buttermilk. Serve right away sprinkled with chives or sliced green onions.

MAKES: 4 to 6 servings

PREPARATION TIME: 15 minutes / COOKING TIME: 25 minutes

Nutrients per serving: 4.9 g protein, 0.6 g total fat (0.2 g saturated, 1 mg cholesterol), 41.8 g carbohydrates, 0.9 mg iron, 74 mg calcium, 286 mg sodium, 3.4 g fibre, 186 calories

Excellent source of vitamin B6.
Good source of thiamine, niacin and magnesium.
Moderate amount of dietary fibre.

Health Wonders

Vitamin D and Absorption

Calcium may be the essential, all-star bone-building material, but don't forget vitamin D, which is necessary for the effective absorption of calcium from your diet. Without it, your body is capable of absorbing only 10 to 15 percent of the calcium you consume. Once calcium is absorbed, vitamin D also plays a role in depositing the nutrient in your bones and teeth.

We most often get vitamin D from exposure to the sun – it isn't present in many foods and our bodies don't store it. While milk and soy beverages have been fortified with vitamin D, yogurt and cheese are not. Some fatty fish, egg yolk, butter and margarine are also good sources of vitamin D.

Calcium: Your Daily Dose

The Osteoporosis Society of Canada recommends 1,000 mg a day of calcium for females between the ages of 19 and 49 with an increase of up to 500 mg per day after 50. Here are some easy ways to get calcium from low-fat dairy:

  1 cup (250 mL) milk, whether whole or skim, contains 315 mg
  1.7 oz (50 g) cheese, such as brick or cheddar,
    contains 350 mg
  ¾ cup (175 mL) plain yogurt contains 292 mg

Taking It All In
The calcium that naturally occurs in food is not always completely absorbed by our bodies. Some of the factors that hinder absorption are a daily intake of more than two glasses of alcohol, eating more than 2 to 3 oz (60 to 90 g) of animal protein at a meal, drinking more than 3 cups of caffeine-containing beverages such as coffee, tea and cola drinks a day, smoking and too much salt.

Buttermilk

Buttermilk is an unfortunate name for a wonderful product. Many people think it's high in fat, but it's actually the opposite. Buttermilk was the name given to the liquid formed when cow's milk was churned in the farmhouse to make butter. Today, most buttermilk is made by adding a bacterial culture to partially skimmed milk, giving a surprisingly rich-tasting but low-fat milk.

Do not substitute buttermilk for regular milk called for in a recipe because buttermilk is more acidic and will adversely affect the workings of the baking powder or baking soda that make your baked goods rise.

Mock Light Béarnaise Sauce

If you adore the richness of fish or vegetables smothered with Béarnaise sauce but shy away from it because of the calories, then you'll love this no-cook version made with a yogurt base. Simply divine!

½ cup	low-fat yogurt or light sour cream	125 mL
¼ cup	warm water	50 mL
2 tbsp	finely minced shallots or sweet onion	30 mL
2 tsp	freshly squeezed lemon juice	10 mL
1 tbsp	olive oil	15 mL
1 tbsp	finely chopped fresh tarragon or ½ tsp (2 mL) dried tarragon	15 mL
⅛ to ¼ tsp	each of salt and freshly ground white pepper	0.5 to 1 mL

1. Whisk yogurt with water, shallots, lemon juice, oil, tarragon and ⅛ teaspoon (0.5 mL) each of salt and pepper. Taste and add more salt and pepper, if needed. Use right away at room temperature; however, flavour improves if covered and refrigerated overnight. Refrigerated sauce will keep well for up to 2 days. Sauce is great served over salmon steaks or on eggs Benedict made with smoked salmon. Layer smoked salmon on a toasted English muffin. Top with a hot poached egg, then drizzle with room-temperature sauce.

MAKES: about 1 cup (250 mL)

PREPARATION TIME: 10 minutes

Nutrients per tablespoon (15 mL): 0.4 g protein, 1 g total fat (0.2 g saturated, 0 mg cholesterol), 0.8 g carbohydrates, 15 mg calcium, 24 mg sodium, 0 g fibre, 13 calories

California Buttermilk-and-Herb Marinated Chicken

This low-fat grilled chicken is ultra moist and full flavoured. It's also ideal for grilling ahead for a family picnic — and a lot lower in calories than fried chicken.

1 cup	buttermilk	250 mL
	finely grated peel and juice of 1 large lemon	
2 tbsp	liquid honey	30 mL
1 tsp	dried leaf oregano	5 mL
1 tsp	dried basil	5 mL
1 tsp	salt	5 mL
½ tsp	freshly ground black pepper	2 mL
6	medium-size skinless, boneless chicken breasts	6

1. In a large bowl, stir buttermilk with lemon peel and juice, honey, oregano, basil, salt and pepper. Place chicken in a heavy-duty plastic bag and pour marinade over top. Seal as close to chicken as possible. Place bag in bowl. Refrigerate for at least 8 hours or overnight. Turn chicken partway through this time.

2. When ready to barbecue, grease grill, then preheat barbecue to medium. Remove chicken from marinade and discard marinade. Place chicken on barbecue. Grill with lid closed, turning occasionally, until chicken feels springy, from 15 to 20 minutes.

MAKES: 6 servings
PREPARATION TIME: 5 minutes / MARINATING TIME: 8 hours
GRILLING TIME: 15 minutes

Nutrients per serving: 32.6 g protein, 2.1 g total fat (0.6 saturated, 84 mg cholesterol), 1.9 g carbohydrates, 0.6 mg iron, 17 mg calcium, 167 mg sodium, 0 g fibre, 165 calories

Excellent source of niacin and vitamin B6.
Good source of vitamin B12.

beta carotene

calcium

vitamin B

Leafy greens

folic acid

Dark green leafy vegetables, such as spinach, kale and Swiss chard, are our best sources of folic acid, a B vitamin important for women planning pregnancy and during because it reduces the risk of neural tube defects. They also lower blood levels of homocysteine, a substance which can damage arterial walls. They are also a rich source of luteins, an antioxidant that may lower the risk of macula degeneration, a leading cause of irreversible blindness in seniors.

luteins

Strawberry and Spinach Salad with Sugared Almonds

If you're a fan of Stuart McLean's "Vinyl Café" on CBC Radio, you may be familiar with this nutrient-packed salad that he first tasted during a visit to Sioux Lookout in Ontario.

¼ cup	vegetable oil	50 mL
2 tbsp	raspberry vinegar or red wine vinegar	30 mL
1 tbsp	Worcestershire sauce	15 mL
1 tbsp	granulated sugar (optional)	15 mL
2 tsp	poppy seeds	10 mL
1	green onion, finely chopped	1
½ tsp	salt	2 mL
pinch	paprika	pinch
½ cup	slivered almonds	125 mL
¼ cup	granulated sugar	50 mL
2 tsp	water	10 mL
2	(10-oz/284-g) bags spinach or 3 large bunches	2
2 cups	sliced strawberries	500 mL

1. Place dressing ingredients from oil to paprika in a jar. Seal and shake. Leave at room temperature up to 1 day or refrigerate 3 days. Oil a large piece of foil and place on counter. Place almonds, sugar and water in a medium-size frying pan. Stir over medium heat until sugar melts. When sugar turns light golden, stir slowly and constantly with a wooden spoon until all sugar is an even golden shade and coats almonds, from 6 to 8 minutes. Immediately turn coated almonds out onto foil. Don't touch. They're extremely hot. When cool, break into small pieces. If kitchen is warm and humid, refrigerate.

2. Wash spinach, discard tough stems, dry. Tear into bite-size pieces. Place in a large bowl with berries. Toss with about half of dressing, then keep adding a little more dressing and tossing until spinach is lightly coated. Add nuts and toss.

MAKES: 8 servings

PREPARATION TIME: 15 minutes / COOKING TIME: 6 minutes

Nutrients per serving: 4 g protein, 11.6 g total fat (1 g saturated, 0 mg cholesterol), 13.2 g carbohydrates, 2.4 mg iron, 102 mg calcium, 219 mg sodium, 3.2 g fibre, 162 calories

Excellent source of vitamins A and C, and folic acid.
Good source of iron.
Moderate amount of dietary fibre.

Swiss Chard-Pork Tenderloin Toss

Swiss chard is rising in popularity and not just because of its appealing slightly bitter taste, but because it's high in the cancer-fighting antioxidant beta carotene. This intriguing but easy stir-fry will appeal to everyone at the dinner table. Toss with chow mein noodles or mound on rice.

1	bunch Swiss chard or 10-oz (284-g) bag spinach or 1 bok choy	1
1	red pepper	1
1	pork tenderloin, about ¾ lb (375 g)	1
2 tsp	vegetable oil	10 mL
1 tsp	sesame oil	5 mL
¼ cup	orange juice or chicken broth	50 mL
1 tsp	cornstarch	5 mL
2 tbsp	each of soy sauce and liquid honey	30 mL
1 tbsp	grated fresh ginger or 1 tsp (5 mL) bottled minced ginger	15 mL
2	minced garlic cloves	2
½ tsp	each of salt and freshly ground black pepper	2 mL

1. Separate Swiss chard leaves and stems. Wash separately, pat dry, then coarsely shred leaves and slice stems into bite-size lengths. If using spinach, discard tough stems, wash leaves and coarsely shred. Or trim root end from bok choy, then slice into bite-size pieces. Cut pepper and pork into thin strips.

2. Heat 1 teaspoon (5 mL) each vegetable and sesame oil in a large wok or frying pan with deep sides over medium-high heat. Add pork and stir-fry until pork changes colour, from 2 to 4 minutes. Remove from pan. Meanwhile, in a small bowl, stir juice with cornstarch, soy, honey, ginger and garlic.

3. Add remaining teaspoon (5 mL) oil to pan, then add Swiss chard stems and red pepper. Stir-fry for 2 minutes. Stir in Swiss chard or spinach leaves or bok choy. Stir juice mixture and pour into pan. Add pork and stir until sauce has thickened slightly, from 2 to 3 minutes. Taste and add up to 1 tablespoon (15 mL) more soy sauce, if you like. You may also want to add salt and black pepper and a drizzle of sesame oil.

MAKES: 2 to 4 servings

PREPARATION TIME: 8 minutes / COOKING TIME: 6 minutes

Nutrients per serving: 22.6 g protein, 5.7 g total fat (1.1 g saturated, 50 mg cholesterol), 17.3 g carbohydrates, 3 mg iron, 52 mg calcium, 962 mg sodium, 2 g fibre, 208 calories

Excellent source of vitamins A, C, B_6 and B_{12}.
Good source of iron and zinc.
Moderate amount of dietary fibre.

Balsamic-Glazed Peaches, Arugula and Chèvre Salad

Aromatic arugula gives an iron and calcium boost to this pretty salad. Its peppery edge cuts the richness of creamy goat cheese and complements the sweetness of sun-ripened peaches to create an easy-to-prepare sumptuous salad.

1	bunch arugula, about 4 cups (1 L)	1
4 cups	baby spinach	1 L
2	peaches or nectarines, peeled	2
¼ cup	balsamic vinegar	50 mL
3 tbsp	olive oil	45 mL
1	small minced garlic clove	1
¼ tsp	each of salt and freshly ground black pepper	1 mL
½ to ¾ cup	creamy chèvre (goat cheese), about a 3- to 4-oz (101- to 140-g) roll or low-fat feta	125 to 175 mL

1. Wash arugula and spinach, then spin dry. Toss together in a bowl. Slice peaches into wedges and discard pits. Place in a medium-size bowl. In a very small saucepan or frying pan over medium-high heat, bring vinegar to a boil. Boil, uncovered, watching closely until slightly thickened, from 1 to 3 minutes. Drizzle reduced vinegar over peaches and toss gently to coat.

2. In a small bowl, whisk oil with garlic, salt and pepper. If there is any excess vinegar from peaches, drain off and whisk into oil mixture. Drizzle the dressing over arugula and spinach and toss to evenly coat. Place a nest of greens on each salad plate. Arrange glazed peaches on greens, then crumble 2 tablespoons (30 mL) cheese over each salad.

MAKES: 6 servings

PREPARATION TIME: 10 minutes / COOKING TIME: 3 minutes

Nutrients per serving: 4.9 g protein, 10.1 g total fat (3 g saturated, 7 mg cholesterol), 8.8 g carbohydrates, 1.9 mg iron, 118 mg calcium, 187 mg sodium, 2 g fibre, 139 calories

Excellent source of vitamin A and folic acid. **Good source of** vitamin C and magnesium. **Moderate amount of** dietary fibre.

Health Wonders

Folic Acid

Folic acid reduces the risk of heart disease, birth defects and research shows that it may also cut women's cancer risk. In a study published in the *Annals of Internal Medicine* in 1999, doctors followed 90,000 female nurses for 15 years, who were taking folic acid, a B-complex vitamin found in leafy green vegetables such as spinach and Brussels sprouts. Women who took 400 micrograms (the recommended amount) of folic acid daily in multivitamin supplements for 15 years had a 75 percent decrease in colon cancer risk. According to Canadian cancer statistics, about 2,900 women die of colorectal cancer a year. Folic acid taken in vitamin form had a stronger effect on reducing cancer risk than when it was consumed in food.

B There

Drinking alcohol increases your risk of developing breast cancer. If you imbibe and have a low intake of folic acid, the B vitamin found in leafy green vegetables, you're at even greater risk.

Cultivating Variety

Leafy green vegetables such as Swiss chard and rapini are rising in popularity not just because of their visual appeal but also because they're high in the antioxidant beta carotene, which is believed to protect against cancer. So when fatigue caused by eating the same old thing hits, try some of the following suggestions to revitalize your interest in eating your veggies. Use mesclun to replace lettuce or spinach in your favourite salads – or simply toss with equal amounts of olive oil and balsamic vinegar. Raw kolhrabi makes a nice crudité and is also delicious shredded and sautéed in butter. Treat Swiss chard as you would spinach, cooking it only with the water that clings to it after washing, just until it wilts. (Also see Salad Days, page 39).

Hot Asian Beef Salad on Cool Greens

Mesclun is a colourful mixture of small, young salad greens that includes arugula, radicchio and baby spinach. Here we've paired it with the exotic flavours of the Orient for an easy main-course salad.

6 cups	mixed salad greens, such as mesclun greens	1.5 L
1	large sweet red pepper	1
1 cup	bean sprouts	250 mL
½ lb	lean ground beef, chicken or turkey	250 g
⅓ cup	Japanese or miso salad dressing	75 mL
	or ¼ cup (50 mL) vinaigrette-style Caesar salad	
	dressing whisked with 2 tbsp (30 mL) teriyaki sauce	

1. Place salad greens in a large shallow bowl. Halve pepper and remove seeds and white membranes. Slice into thin strips. Add to bowl along with bean sprouts. Refrigerate just until meat mixture is ready or up to 1 day.

2. Place beef in a large non-stick frying pan over medium-high heat. Using back of a spoon or fork, break up meat. Cook, stirring often and adding a little oil to pan, if necessary, to prevent sticking, until meat is lightly browned, from 7 to 10 minutes. Drain off any excess fat, then stir in 2 tablespoons (30 mL) salad dressing.

3. Immediately drizzle remaining salad dressing over lettuce mixture. Toss gently until well combined. Add beef mixture, toss and serve immediately. Terrific with focaccia or nan bread or serve in crusty rolls or warm tortillas.

MAKES: 4 to 6 servings

PREPARATION TIME: 10 minutes / COOKING TIME: 7 minutes

Nutrients per serving: 9.1 g protein, 8 g total fat (1.8 g saturated, 19 mg cholesterol), 5.8 g carbohydrates, 1.4 mg iron, 50 mg calcium, 369 mg sodium, 1.4 g fibre, 128 calories

Excellent source of vitamins A, C and B12, and folic acid.
Good source of niacin and zinc.

Peppery Greens with Maple Dressing

Serve this light salad after the main course to cleanse everyone's palate and set the stage for dessert.

6 cups	each of arugula and curly endive or 12 cups (3 L) mesclun greens	1.5 L
4 cups	torn radicchio	1 L
3 tbsp	cider vinegar	45 mL
2 tbsp	maple syrup	30 mL
	finely grated peel of half an orange	
1½ tsp	Dijon mustard	7 mL
½ tsp	salt	2 mL
½ tsp	freshly ground black pepper	2 mL
⅓ cup	extra-virgin olive oil	75 mL

1. Wash greens and radicchio well. Spin or pat dry with paper towels. Tear into bite-size pieces. Place in a bowl or refrigerate in tightly sealed plastic bags for up to 2 days. In a measuring cup or jar, combine vinegar, syrup, peel, mustard, salt and pepper. While whisking, drizzle in oil. If not using right away, cover and leave at room temperature for up to 1 day or refrigerate up to 5 days.

2. Before serving, place greens and radicchio in a salad bowl. For a warm salad, heat dressing in microwave on high for 30 seconds or until steaming. Stir, then drizzle half over salad while tossing. Add more dressing as needed. A warm dressing brings out more flavour, but it's also good at room temperature. Add salt and pepper to taste.

MAKES: 8 to 10 servings

PREPARATION TIME: 15 minutes / MICROWAVE TIME: 30 seconds

Nutrients per serving: 1.5 g protein, 7.5 g total fat (1 g saturated, 0 mg cholesterol), 6.1 g carbohydrates, 0.9 mg iron, 78 mg calcium, 144 mg sodium, 1.3 g fibre, 93 calories

Excellent source of folic acid.

Featherlight Green Salad with Citrus Vinaigrette

This delicate and refreshing salad is perfect for balancing the spicy flavours of curried rice and other robust main-course dishes.

1 tsp	each of freshly squeezed lemon and lime juice	5 mL
2 tsp	liquid honey or granulated sugar	10 mL
¼ tsp	each of salt and freshly ground black pepper	1 mL
¼ cup	extra-virgin olive oil	50 mL
12 cups	curly leaf lettuce or mesclun greens	3 L
1 tbsp	toasted sesame seeds (see Tip, below)	15 mL

1. In a small bowl, whisk lemon juice with lime juice, honey, salt and pepper. Whisking constantly, drizzle in olive oil. Taste and add a little more juice, if you like. Make dressing up to 2 days ahead and leave at room temperature or refrigerate.

2. Wash and spin dry lettuce or wrap in paper towel to dry. Tear into bite-size pieces. Place in a large salad bowl. If not using right away, cover with a damp towel and refrigerate for up to half a day. Just before serving, toss with dressing. Sprinkle with sesame seeds and serve immediately.

MAKES: 8 servings

PREPARATION TIME: 5 minutes

TIP: To toast sesame seeds, spread them out in an even layer on a cake pan or pie plate. Toast in a preheated 350°F (180°C) oven until golden, about 5 minutes.

Nutrients per serving: 1.4 g protein, 7.6 g total fat (1 g saturated, 0 mg cholesterol), 4.6 g carbohydrates, 1.3 mg iron, 59 mg calcium, 80 mg sodium, 1.3 g fibre, 87 calories

Good source of vitamin A and folic acid.

Health Wonders

Salad Days

Arugula has an assertive peppery-mustard taste. Though popular in Italy for generations where it's often called rocket, we're just now coming to appreciate the wallop of flavour it gives when tossed in a salad, pasta, risotto or soup. This green is sold in small bunches, often with roots attached, and is very perishable. Refrigerate it in a plastic bag and use within a day or two.

Mesclun is a mixture of small, young salad greens, such as baby spinach, frisée, arugula, oak leaf and radicchio, that deliver a mix of bitter and tangy flavours. It's often labelled as "salad mix" or "baby greens" and sold loose by the pound or kilogram in grocery produce sections. For an economical but still interesting approach, mix an equal amount of mesclun greens with torn Boston, leaf, Bibb or romaine lettuce. Unless sold packaged and labelled "ready to use," mesclun should be washed and spun- or blot-dried before using.

Spinach is a good source of beta carotene and is also one of the best sources of lutein, a phytochemical that helps prevent cataracts and damage to the macula, the small sensitive area of the retina that's responsible for central vision. One cup (250 mL) of cooked spinach has just 40 calories and more than 100 percent of our recommended daily intake for vitamin A and folic acid.

The dark green colour is an indication of spinach's powerhouse of nutrients, including vitamins A, B, C and E, and it is also a source of dietary fibre. Raw spinach is rich in iron, but when it's cooked, the oxalic acid blocks some of the absorption of both its iron and calcium. A little vitamin C, even a squirt of lemon or orange juice, improves absorption.

Swiss chard is related to beets, with a spinach-like appearance and tastes like a cross between the two – earthy, slightly sweet and sometimes with bitter undertones. It's a good source of iron and vitamins A and C. Choose chard that has firm stalks and evenly coloured leaves. Use it within a few days of purchase, as it doesn't keep well. Cook stems separately. The French have a passion for braising them. The leaves take longer to cook than spinach but suit most preparations that call for spinach. Italians use Swiss chard to stuff pasta, fortify soups and they also sauté it alone in olive oil with lemon juice. Small baby chard adds character to a tossed salad.

Stir-Fried Vegetable Egg Scramble

If you're not sure what to make for dinner and you don't feel like doing a lot of cooking, this satisfying quick-to-prepare supper fits the bill.

1 tbsp	olive or vegetable oil	15 mL
2	carrots, thinly sliced on a diagonal	2
1	green pepper, cut into thin strips	1
¼ cup	teriyaki sauce	50 mL
3 cups	thinly sliced bok choy, about 3 to 4 stalks	750 mL
4	eggs	4
2	green onions, thinly sliced	2

1. Prepare and measure out all ingredients before beginning to cook. Heat oil in a wok or large frying pan over medium-high. Add carrots and pepper and stir-fry for 1 minute. Add teriyaki sauce. Cook, stirring often until vegetables are tender-crisp, from 5 to 6 minutes. Add bok choy and continue cooking, from 2 to 3 more minutes.

2. Make a well in the centre of vegetables and break in eggs. Keeping the eggs as best you can in the centre of the well, stir briskly until eggs are scrambled as you like. Sprinkle with green onion. Mix with vegetables or serve vegetables on the side.

MAKES: 2 servings

PREPARATION TIME: 10 minutes / COOKING TIME: 10 minutes

Nutrients per serving: 18 g protein, 17.2 g total fat (4.1 g saturated, 429 mg cholesterol), 21.7 g carbohydrates, 4.2 mg iron, 202 mg calcium, 1,599 mg sodium, 5.1 g fibre, 307 calories

Excellent source of vitamins A, C, B6 and B12, and folic acid and iron.
Good source of calcium.
High amount of dietary fibre.

Sesame Stir-Fried Asparagus, Spinach and Red Onion

This high-fibre recipe pairs spinach and tender asparagus with the tantalizing but not overpowering flavour combo of sesame oil and lemon juice.

1	large bunch asparagus, about 1 lb (500 g)	1
1	small red onion	1
1	large bunch spinach	1
1 tbsp	butter	15 mL
½ tsp	dark sesame oil	2 mL
2	minced garlic cloves	2
½ tsp	salt	2 mL
¼ cup	chopped fresh mint or coriander	50 mL
1 tbsp	lemon or lime juice or balsamic vinegar	15 mL

1. Trim asparagus. Slice into 2-inch (5-cm) pieces. Slice onion in half, then slice into half-rounds. Discard tough stems from spinach. Wash leaves and dry, leaving slightly damp.

2. Heat butter and sesame oil in a large frying pan over medium-high heat. Add onion and garlic. Stir-fry for 3 minutes, reducing heat to medium if onion starts to brown. Add asparagus and 1 tablespoon (15 mL) water. Sprinkle with salt. Stir-fry until onion is soft and asparagus is tender-crisp, about 3 minutes. Add damp spinach and stir-fry until wilted, from 1 to 2 minutes. Stir in mint and lemon juice. Taste and add additional mint or lemon juice, if you like.

MAKES: 4 servings

PREPARATION TIME: 15 minutes / COOKING TIME: 8 minutes

Nutrients per serving: 5 g protein, 4 g total fat (2 g saturated, 8 mg cholesterol), 13.5 g carbohydrates, 3.1 mg iron, 126 mg calcium, 372 mg sodium, 4.4 g fibre, 97 calories

Excellent source of vitamin A and folic acid. **Good source of** vitamins C and B6, and iron. **High amount of** dietary fibre.

Easy Chicken and Greens Sauté

Bok choy, a delicate vegetable you probably first tasted in a Chinese stir-fry, is an easily absorbed source of calcium. Here we've paired it with chicken and carrots for a swift sauté and a brief braise. The perfect results are tender chicken and flavourful vegetables with an Oriental twist. Top with a healthy sprinkle of calcium-rich sesame seeds.

8	skinless, boneless chicken thighs or 4 skinless, boneless breasts	8
2	large garlic cloves	2
1	large head bok choy or broccoli	1
1 tbsp	olive oil	15 mL
¼ cup	all-purpose flour	50 mL
½ cup	white wine or chicken broth	125 mL
½ tsp	hot red chili flakes	2 mL
½ tsp	salt	2 mL
2 cups	baby carrots	500 mL
2 tsp	dark sesame oil	10 mL
2 tbsp	toasted sesame seeds (see Tip, page 38)	30 mL

1. Remove fat from chicken and discard. Thinly slice garlic. Thickly slice bok choy or cut broccoli into florets. You should have about 4 cups (1 L).

2. Heat oil in a large frying pan over medium heat. Dip chicken into flour and shake off excess. Then sauté until lightly golden, about 5 minutes per side. Add garlic, then wine or broth, red chili flakes and salt. Bring to boil and add carrots. Partially cover and reduce heat to low. Simmer 10 minutes for breasts or 15 minutes for thighs, until chicken is almost springy to the touch, turning chicken partway through. Add bok choy or broccoli and sesame oil. Continue simmering, uncovered and stirring often, until vegetables are done as you like, from 5 to 10 more minutes. Sprinkle with sesame seeds. For a more concentrated sauce, remove chicken and vegetables to a heated serving plate. Boil broth until reduced to about ½ cup (125 mL). Pour over chicken and serve with rice or pasta.

MAKES: 4 servings

PREPARATION TIME: 20 minutes / COOKING TIME: 30 minutes

Nutrients per serving: 25.7 g protein, 14.4 g total fat (2.7 g saturated, 95 mg cholesterol), 13.1 g carbohydrates, 3.1 mg iron, 113 mg calcium, 452 mg sodium, 3.1 g fibre, 291 calories

Excellent source of vitamins A and B6, and folic acid.
Good source of vitamin C and iron.
Moderate amount of dietary fibre.

Baby Bok Choy Sauté

Baby bok choy is even more delicately flavoured than regular bok choy, with just a hint of sweet cabbage taste — all the right stuff to make it a sophisticated side dish to a trendy entrée. Its deep green leaves have thick white stalks that become surprisingly tender when briefly braised.

1 cup	chicken broth or bouillon	250 mL
¼ tsp	hot red chili flakes	1 mL
1	large minced garlic clove or 1 tsp (5 mL) bottled minced garlic	1
4	baby bok choy	4

1. In a large frying pan over medium heat, bring broth, chili flakes and garlic to a boil. Trim base from bok choy, then add whole baby bok choy to broth. Reduce heat so mixture just simmers. Cook, uncovered, for 5 minutes. Turn bok choy and continue cooking another 5 minutes. Serve with a little broth spooned over top.

Bok choy: If baby bok choy is not available, coarsely slice 1 regular bok choy. Add to boiling broth and simmer, uncovered and stirring often, until tender, about 10 minutes.

MAKES: 4 servings

PREPARATION TIME: 10 minutes / COOKING TIME: 10 minutes

Nutrients per serving: 3.2 g protein, 0.6 g total fat (0.1 g saturated, 0 mg cholesterol), 2.8 g carbohydrates, 1.4 mg iron, 118 mg calcium, 236 mg sodium, 2 g fibre, 26 calories

Excellent source of vitamins A and C.
Good source of folic acid.
Moderate amount of dietary fibre.

complex
carbohydrates

iron

protein

Legumes

A legume is a seed pod that splits on two sides when ripe. This group includes soybeans, chickpeas, navy and kidney beans, peas and lentils, as well as peanuts and carob. They're spectacularly good for us as they're rich in complex carbohydrates and are our best source of plant protein – which takes on increased importance as we move toward more meatless meals. They are also a good source of fibre and most are low in fat.

Five-Star Bean Soup

We've jazzed up this wholesome soup with beta carotene-rich vegetables and fiery cayenne.

1¼ cups	mixed dried beans, such as Romano, black beans, navy, red or white kidney and/or pinto	300 mL
¼ cup	each of barley, lentils and split peas	50 mL
1	minced garlic clove	1
2	onions, chopped	2
2	large carrots, chopped	2
2	celery stalks, chopped	2
8 cups	chicken broth or bouillon or water	2 L
28-oz	can tomatoes, including juice	796-mL
¼ tsp	dried leaf thyme	1 mL
1	bay leaf	1
¼ tsp	freshly ground black pepper	1 mL
¼ tsp	cayenne pepper	1 mL
1	sweet red or green pepper, seeded and chopped	1
½ cup	chopped fresh parsley or coriander (optional)	125 mL

1. Place beans in a large saucepan and generously cover with water. Bring to a boil, uncovered, over high heat. Remove from heat, cover and let soak for 1 hour. Then drain beans. Measure barley, lentils and peas into a sieve. Rinse under cold water and drain.

2. In a large saucepan, combine garlic, onions, carrots and celery. (If you like crunchy vegetables in your soup, save half of carrots and celery to add near end of cooking.) Add broth, tomatoes and juice, seasonings, beans and barley mixture. Break up tomatoes with a fork. Bring to a boil, skimming off any foam. Cover and reduce heat to low. Simmer, stirring occasionally, until all beans are tender, from 2 to 2½ hours.

3. Stir in any reserved vegetables and pepper. Continue simmering until done as you like, about 5 minutes. Add chopped parsley. Taste and add more seasonings or a squeeze of lemon juice, if needed. Serve with whole grain bread and a green salad. Covered and refrigerated, soup will keep well for up to 3 days or freeze.

MAKES: 14 cups

PREPARATION TIME: 20 minutes / SOAKING TIME: 1 hour / COOKING TIME: 2 hours

Nutrients per cup (250 mL): 9.6 g protein, 1.4 g total fat (0.3 g saturated, 0 mg cholesterol), 24.3 g carbohydrates, 2.5 mg iron, 55 mg calcium, 553 mg sodium, 5.4 g fibre, 144 calories

Excellent source of vitamin A and folic acid.
Good source of vitamin C.
High amount of dietary fibre.

Chickpea, Jalapeño and Roasted Red Pepper Salad

With a squirt of lime juice and a hit of heat, this no-fat-added salad has plenty of zip. We've even given pantry options for all the ingredients.

19-oz	can chickpeas or 2 cups (500 mL) cooked chickpeas	540-mL
1	large sweet red pepper, roasted and seeded or ½ (10-oz/340-g) jar drained roasted red peppers	1
2	jalapeño peppers or ½ (4.5-oz/127-g) can drained diced green chilies	2
¼ cup	chopped fresh basil or coriander or ½ tsp (2 mL) dried basil	50 mL
2 tsp	freshly squeezed lime or lemon juice or balsamic or tarragon vinegar	10 mL

1. Drain canned chickpeas, rinse with cold water and drain again. Place in a mixing bowl. Coarsely chop red pepper. Seed and finely chop jalapeños. Add both to chickpeas. Sprinkle with basil. Stir until mixed. Add lime juice and toss. Then add salt and pepper, if needed.

MAKES: 2 cups
PREPARATION TIME: 10 minutes

Nutrients per cup (250 mL): 14.6 g protein, 3.3 g total fat (0.3 g saturated, 0 mg cholesterol), 50.2 g carbohydrates, 2.3 mg iron, 61 mg calcium, 411 mg sodium, 7.5 g fibre, 278 calories

Excellent source of vitamins A, C and B6, and folic acid.
Good source of iron.
Very high amount of dietary fibre.

Colourful Carrot and Lentil Soup

Prepare this flavourful and nutrient-packed soup in just half an hour. For a vegetarian version, use your own homemade vegetable broth.

½ lb	red lentils, about 1½ cups (375 mL)	250 g
5 cups	chicken or vegetable bouillon, broth or water	1.25 L
½	large onion, chopped	½
3	minced garlic cloves or 1½ tsp (7 mL) bottled minced garlic	3
1½ tsp	ground cumin	7 mL
½ tsp	ground coriander	2 mL
½ tsp	paprika	2 mL
1	bay leaf	1
3	medium-sized carrots	3
1	small sweet red pepper, cored	1
1	green onion, thinly sliced	1
2 tbsp	finely chopped coriander	30 mL
1 to 2 tbsp	freshly squeezed lemon juice	15 to 30 mL
¼ tsp	freshly ground black pepper	1 mL

1. In a large saucepan, combine lentils and bouillon. Bring to a boil over high heat. Skim away any froth. Then stir in onion, garlic, cumin, ground coriander, paprika and bay leaf. Reduce heat to medium-low and simmer, covered.

2. Dice carrots and peppers. Carrots should measure about 1 cup (250 mL). Immediately stir into soup. Continue simmering, covered, until carrots are very tender, about 15 minutes. Lentils in soup will need a total of about 20 minutes to cook. Stir in green onions, fresh coriander, lemon juice and pepper. Remove bay leaf. Serve immediately or refrigerate, covered, for 2 to 3 days or freeze.

MAKES: 7 cups (1.75 L)

PREPARATION TIME: 10 minutes / COOKING TIME: 20 minutes

Nutrients per cup (250 mL): 12.8 g protein, 1.6 g total fat (0.4 g saturated, 0 mg cholesterol), 25.5 g carbohydrates, 4.2 mg iron, 47 mg calcium, 580 mg sodium, 5.3 g fibre, 163 calories

Excellent source of vitamin A, folic acid and iron.
Good source of vitamin C.
High amount of dietary fibre.

White Turkey Chili

While this chili is hearty and bursting with flavour, it's also packed with protein and an amazing source of vitamin C and folic acid.

1 lb	ground turkey or chicken	500 g
1	large onion, chopped	1
2	minced garlic cloves	2
10-oz	can undiluted chicken broth	284-mL
¾ cup	water	175 mL
2 tsp	ground cumin	10 mL
¼ cup	all-purpose flour	50 mL
4.5-oz	can diced green chilies	127-g
¼ tsp	each of salt and freshly ground black pepper	1 mL
2	(19-oz/540-mL) cans white kidney beans	2
2	large yellow, orange or red bell peppers, chopped	2
3	tomatoes, seeded and chopped	3
½ cup	chopped fresh coriander or parsley	125 mL

1. In a large saucepan over medium heat, simmer ground turkey, onion and garlic in ¼ cup (50 mL) broth until turkey loses its pink colour and onion has softened, about 4 minutes. Stir often with a fork to keep turkey separated. Sprinkle turkey with cumin and flour. Stir until turkey and onion are evenly coated. Slowly stir remaining broth and water into saucepan. Bring to a boil over high heat, stirring occasionally. Reduce heat to low. Then stir in entire contents of the can of chilies, salt and pepper. Cover and simmer for 15 minutes, stirring often, to develop flavour.

2. Stir in rinsed kidney beans and chopped bell peppers. Increase heat to medium and cook, stirring occasionally, until hot, about 7 minutes. Stir in tomatoes and coriander just before serving. Taste and add more seasoning, if you wish. This chili is great served with tortilla chips and bowls of sliced green onions and grated orange cheddar to sprinkle over top. Chili can be refrigerated for up to 3 days or freeze.

Make ahead: Prepare chili, but do not add coriander and tomatoes. Chili can be refrigerated for up to 3 days or frozen. After reheating chili, stir in chopped coriander and tomatoes.

MAKES: 9 cups (2.25 L)

PREPARATION TIME: 25 minutes / COOKING TIME: 30 minutes

Nutrients per cup (250 mL): 18.7 g protein, 5.4 g total fat (1.3 g saturated, 33 mg cholesterol), 27.3 g carbohydrates, 2.7 mg iron, 47 mg calcium, 756 mg sodium, 8.9 g fibre, 229 calories

Excellent source of vitamin C and folic acid.
Good source of vitamin B$_6$ and iron.
Very high amount of dietary fibre.

Fiesta Bean Salad

Here's a lower-fat version of a summer favourite filled with colourful peppers. Use whatever cans of beans you have on hand. There's enough protein from the beans that two cups (500 mL) of this salad will fill about one-quarter of your protein needs for the day.

2	(19-oz/540 mL) cans chickpeas or beans, such as mixed, kidney or Romano	2
3	sweet peppers, preferably 1 each of red, yellow and green	3
4	large plum tomatoes	4
4	green onions	4
½ cup	chopped fresh coriander or parsley	125 mL
¼ cup	red wine vinegar	50 mL
3 tsp	ground cumin	15 mL
2 tsp	chili powder	10 mL
½ tsp	salt	2 mL
2	minced garlic cloves	2
2 tbsp	olive oil	30 mL

1. Drain chickpeas or beans into a sieve or colander. Then rinse under cold running water and drain well. Place in a large mixing bowl. Seed and finely chop peppers and tomatoes. Thinly slice onions. Add to chickpeas along with coriander and gently mix.

2. In a small bowl, whisk vinegar with cumin, chili powder, salt and garlic. When thoroughly blended, slowly drizzle in oil while whisking constantly. Pour over chickpea mixture and gently mix to avoid breaking up chickpeas. Serve right away or cover and refrigerate up to 2 days. Flavours mingle and improve as salad stands. Garnish with crisp tortilla chips and pieces of coriander.

MAKES: 10 cups (2.5 L)

PREPARATION TIME: 30 minutes

Nutrients per cup (250 mL): 6.3 g protein, 4.4 g total fat (0.5 g saturated, 0 mg cholesterol), 22.5 g carbohydrates, 1.7 mg iron, 36 mg calcium, 289 mg sodium, 3.6 g fibre, 147 calories

Excellent source of vitamin C.
Good source of vitamin B6 and folic acid.
Moderate amount of dietary fibre.

Amazing Veggie Burgers

It's tough to make a good-tasting vegetarian burger that doesn't require a long list of unusual ingredients and a lot of work. We think we've hit the mark with this burger, which is firm enough to hold together on the barbecue. The patties freeze beautifully, so make a double batch and you'll have some on hand to pull out for the vegetarians in your family.

19-oz	can black beans	540-mL
	or 2 cups (500 mL) cooked black beans	
½ cup	shredded Monterey Jack or mozzarella cheese	125 mL
½ cup	store-bought dry bread crumbs	125 mL
⅓ cup	all-purpose flour	75 mL
1	onion, coarsely chopped	1
1	minced garlic clove	1
1	egg	1
2 tbsp	barbecue sauce or ketchup	30 mL
1 tbsp	Worcestershire sauce	15 mL
1 tsp	vegetable oil	5 mL
½ tsp	each of salt and black pepper	2 mL
½ tsp	barbecue sauce	2 mL
6	sliced hamburger buns (optional)	6

1. Oil grill and preheat barbecue to medium-high heat. Rinse drained canned beans with cold water and drain well. In a food processor, combine beans, cheese, bread crumbs, flour, onion, garlic, egg, barbecue and Worcestershire sauces, oil, salt and pepper. Pulse just until beans are coarsely chopped.

2. Divide mixture into 6 equal portions and, using lightly floured hands, shape into round patties about ½ inch (1 cm) thick. Lightly brush tops of patties with barbecue sauce.

3. Carefully place patties brushed-side down on grill. Brush tops with barbecue sauce and barbecue patties with lid down, turning once and brushing as needed, until well browned and firm, from 8 to 10 minutes. Place buns, if using, cut-side down on grill and toast lightly. Place patties on buns and dress with toppings such as sliced tomatoes, onions and salsa.

MAKES: 6 burgers

PREPARATION TIME: 5 minutes / GRILLING TIME: 8 minutes

Nutrients per burger: 11.2 g protein, 5.5 g total fat (2.3 g saturated, 44 mg cholesterol), 29.5 g carbohydrates, 2.5 mg iron, 119 mg calcium, 549 mg sodium, 4.7 g fibre, 210 calories

Excellent source of folic acid.
Good source of iron, niacin and thiamine.
High amount of dietary fibre.

Fabulous Falafels

In the Middle East, this is fast food. Street vendors fry chickpea balls, then tuck them into a pita with a colourful salad. For a final flourish, they add a squirt or two of tahini and spicy harissa sauces. We've switched ours from the deep-fat fryer to the sauté pan with excellent results.

2	(19-oz/540-mL) cans chickpeas, drained	2
1	egg, beaten	1
¼ cup	all-purpose flour	50 mL
¼ tsp	baking powder	1 mL
1	large onion, finely chopped	1
½ cup	finely chopped fresh parsley or coriander	125 mL
3	minced garlic cloves	3
1½ tsp	each of ground cumin and coriander	7 mL
¾ tsp	salt	4 mL
¼ tsp	cayenne	1 mL
2 tbsp	vegetable oil	30 mL
8	pitas	8
2	tomatoes, chopped	2
1	small head iceberg lettuce, shredded	1
½	English cucumber, chopped	½
½	Spanish or red onion, thinly sliced	½
	tahini and harissa hot sauce	

1. Mash chickpeas with a fork until crumbly. A food processor makes chickpeas too soft. Stir in egg, flour and baking powder, then onion, parsley, garlic and seasonings. Shape mixture into ½-inch (1-cm) thick patties. Place on waxed paper. You should have about 16 patties.

2. Heat 1 tablespoon (15 mL) oil in a large frying pan over medium heat. Add 5 to 6 patties. Sauté until golden, from 5 to 7 minutes per side. Cover to keep warm. Sauté remaining patties, adding more oil if needed. Open up each pita; tuck in 2 patties. Top with tomatoes, lettuce, cucumber and onion. Drizzle with tahini and/or harissa sauce, which is available in Middle Eastern grocery stores.

MAKES: 8 falafel sandwiches

PREPARATION TIME: 15 minutes / COOKING TIME: 20 minutes

Nutrients per sandwich with 2 tbsp (30 mL) tahini sauce:
17.2 g protein, 14.6 g total fat (1.8 g saturated, 27 mg cholesterol), 65.8 g carbohydrates, 4.6 mg iron, 136 mg calcium, 912 mg sodium, 7.2 g fibre, 453 calories

Excellent source of vitamin B6 and folic acid.
Good source of vitamin C.
Very high amount of dietary fibre.

Health Wonders

Peanut Power

Most people think of peanuts as a nut, but they are, in fact, legumes. They contain a mix of heart-protective nutrients and plant compounds. These include heart-healthy mono- and polyunsaturated fats; vitamin E, a powerful antioxidant that helps protect arterial walls from damage; and arginine, a potent dilator of blood vessel walls, which reduces the risk of blood clots. Because peanut butter is high in fat, keep these recommendations in mind:

• Limit serving sizes to no more than 2 tablespoons (30 mL) of peanut butter (190 calories, 16 grams of fat) or about 15 peanuts (165 calories, 14 grams of fat) at any meal or snack.

• Balance the peanut butter with low-fat foods. For instance, enjoy a peanut butter sandwich with a glass of skim milk and a piece of fruit.

Bean Scene

Chickpeas are a terrific lower-fat vegetarian source of protein, which is essential to our daily health. One cup (250 mL) of cooked chickpeas provides about 16 grams of protein, almost a third of our recommended daily nutrient intake for protein. Beans, such as chickpeas, are packed with complex carbohydrates in the form of soluble fibre, which helps lower blood cholesterol, and insoluble fibre, which helps prevent digestive disorders. Together, these two types of fibre may also be helpful in fighting cancer, heart disease and diabetes.

Lentils have added texture and nutrients to Mediterranean foods for centuries. Ready in as little as 10 minutes, they are a healthy low-fat protein partner for grains and vegetables and are rich in soluble fibre, which can help improve blood sugar levels.

Black beans are very high in iron, fibre and folic acid. They have become very popular because, unlike kidney beans, they maintain an al dente texture after cooking or canning. Add to salads and salsas for a colour contrast to bright veggies.

Natural Gas

Dried legumes are high in sugars that our digestive system cannot break down. These sugars are fermented by beneficial bacteria in the intestine, which leads to flatulence – giving beans the name "musical fruit." But soaking, then cooking the legumes in fresh water will eliminate some of these sugars. Or try an over-the-counter supplement such as Beano, which breaks down the gas-causing complex sugars in beans. Add a few drops to your first spoonful of beans or take in tablet form with your first bite.

Middle Eastern Pilaf

Wendy James is a Saskatoon vegetarian who packs lots of flavour and texture into her pilaf. Fragrant with spices and filled with vegetables, this is one of the best vegetarian dishes we have tasted.

1 tbsp	vegetable oil	15 mL
1	onion, chopped	1
2	minced garlic cloves	2
2	carrots, grated or finely chopped	2
¼ tsp	each of hot red chili flakes, cinnamon and cardamom	1 mL
⅛ tsp	allspice or ground cloves	0.5 mL
¾ cup	dried split green peas or brown lentils	175 mL
2½ cups	vegetable broth or water	625 mL
½ cup	orange juice	125 mL
½ or 1¼ tsp	salt	2 or 6 mL
1¼ cups	long-grain rice, such as basmati	300 mL
½	(10-oz/300-g) bag spinach, stems removed	½
1 tbsp	freshly squeezed lemon juice	15 mL
¼ cup	chopped peanuts, toasted pine nuts or almonds	50 mL
½ cup	chopped dried apricots, raisins, currants or dried cranberries	125 mL

1. Preheat oven to 350°F (180°C). Heat oil over medium heat in a large saucepan or pot that can go into the oven. Add the onion, garlic, carrots, chili flakes, cinnamon and cardamom. Sauté 5 minutes. Meanwhile, place peas in a sieve and rinse with water. Drain. Add to onion with broth and juice. Add ½ teaspoon (2 mL) salt or 1¼ teaspoons (6 mL) salt if using water. Bring to a boil. Then stir in rice.

2. Cover tightly and bake in centre of preheated oven until peas are tender and liquid has been absorbed, 25 to 30 minutes. Meanwhile, wash spinach and drain. You should have about 4 cups (1 L). Tear or cut into small pieces. When rice is ready, stir in lemon juice, then spinach, peanuts and apricots. Cover and let stand 5 minutes to soften dried fruit and wilt spinach. Terrific with steamed carrots.

MAKES: 8 cups (2 L)

PREPARATION TIME: 20 minutes / COOKING TIME: 10 minutes / BAKING TIME: 25 minutes

Nutrients per cup (250 mL): 9.4 g protein, 4.8 g total fat (0.6 g saturated, 0 mg cholesterol), 47 g carbohydrates, 2.2 mg iron, 58 mg calcium, 367 mg sodium, 4.4 g fibre, 263 calories

Excellent source of vitamin A and folic acid.

Good source of iron.

High amount of dietary fibre.

Vegetarian Curry-in-a-Hurry

When a hot and spicy craving comes upon you, satisfy it with this robust and flavourful lower-fat number.

1 tbsp	butter	15 mL
1	onion, chopped	1
2	minced garlic cloves	2
2 tsp	curry powder	10 mL
½ cup	water	125 mL
4	large fresh tomatoes or 8 canned tomatoes	4
19-oz	can lentils	540-mL
½ tsp	salt (optional)	2 mL
½ tsp	sugar (optional)	2 mL
½ cup	light sour cream	125 mL
	chopped fresh coriander (optional)	

1. Melt butter in a large saucepan over medium heat. Add onion and garlic. Sauté until softened, about 5 minutes. Sprinkle with curry powder. Stir for 2 minutes, then add water. Boil gently, uncovered and stirring often until most of liquid evaporates, from 5 to 8 minutes. Meanwhile, seed fresh tomatoes and coarsely chop. (If using canned tomatoes, seeding is not necessary, just coarsely chop.) Rinse and drain canned lentils.

2. When most of liquid is evaporated, stir in tomatoes and lentils. Heat through. Taste and add salt and sugar, if needed. Just before serving, blend in sour cream. Sprinkle with coriander and serve over hot rice or scoop up in a warm tortilla.

MAKES: 4 cups (1 L)

PREPARATION TIME: 10 minutes / COOKING TIME: 15 minutes

Nutrients per cup (250 mL): 13.1 g protein, 5.4 g total fat (2.8 saturated, 12 mg cholesterol), 35.6 g carbohydrates, 4.6 mg iron, 103 mg calcium, 598 mg sodium, 7.1 g fibre, 230 calories

Excellent source of vitamin C, folic acid and iron.
Good source of vitamins A and B6.
Very high amount of dietary fibre.

Chili-Cumin Rice and Bean Skillet Supper

This high-fibre, low-fat vegetarian dish will serve a crowd! Pass bowls of chopped fresh coriander and grated cheddar plus a big basket of crisp tortilla chips.

1 tbsp	vegetable oil	15 mL
1	large onion, peeled and chopped	1
1	large minced garlic clove	1
2	green peppers, seeded and chopped	2
4 tsp	chili powder	20 mL
2 tsp	ground cumin	10 mL
1½ tsp	salt	7 mL
¼ tsp	cayenne pepper	1 mL
1½ cups	uncooked long-grain rice	375 mL
2½ cups	water	625 mL
2	(19-oz/540-mL) cans tomatoes, including juice	2
19-oz	can black or Romano beans, rinsed and drained or 2 cups (500 mL) cooked beans	540-mL
2 cups	frozen or canned corn kernels	500 g

1. Heat oil in a large saucepan over medium heat. Add onion, garlic and half of the peppers. Stir occasionally for 5 minutes. Add spices. Stir constantly, for about 1 minute.

2. Add rice, stirring until coated. Stir in water and tomatoes, including juice. Bring to a boil, stirring frequently. Reduce heat to low, cover and barely simmer for 20 minutes. Add drained beans, remaining peppers and corn. Cover and continue cooking until rice is done as you like, from 15 to 20 minutes.

Meat option: Heat oil in saucepan. Crumble in ½ pound (250 g) lean ground beef or chicken. Increase heat to medium-high. Sauté meat, stirring frequently, until it picks up some browning, about 5 minutes. Then add onion, garlic, peppers. Reduce heat to medium and continue with recipe.

MAKES: 8 to 10 servings

PREPARATION TIME: 15 minutes / COOKING TIME: 45 minutes

Nutrients per serving without meat: 7.4 g protein, 2.3 g total fat (0.2 g saturated, 0 mg cholesterol), 43 g carbohydrates, 1.9 mg iron, 46 mg calcium, 536 mg sodium, 4.7 g fibre, 215 calories

Excellent source of folic acid.
Good source of vitamin C.
High amount of dietary fibre.

Sweet Pepper and Black Bean Stir-Fry

Serve this zesty south-of-the-border stir-fry over rice or wrapped in tortillas for a delicious meatless lunch or dinner.

½	red onion	½
3	sweet peppers, preferably 1 each of red, yellow and green	3
¼ cup	coriander leaves	50 mL
1 tbsp	each of butter and vegetable oil	15 mL
1	minced garlic clove	1
1 tbsp	chili powder	15 mL
¼ tsp	each of salt and freshly ground black pepper	1 mL
1 cup	canned black beans, rinsed and drained	250 mL
½	lime	½
4	tortillas (7-inch/18-cm)	4
½ cup	grated cheddar cheese (optional)	125 mL

1. Before beginning to stir-fry, thinly slice onion and peppers. Then coarsely chop coriander and set aside separately. Heat butter and oil in a deep wide frying pan or wok over medium-high heat until hot but not smoking. Add onion and stir-fry for 2 minutes. Add peppers and garlic. Sprinkle with chili powder, salt and pepper and stir-fry until onion starts to brown, from 3 to 5 minutes.

2. Stir in coriander and beans and stir-fry until heated through, from 1 to 2 minutes. Squeeze juice from lime over top and toss to mix.

3. Place about ½ cup (125 mL) pepper mixture in centre of each tortilla shell. Sprinkle with about 2 tablespoons (30 mL) cheese, then roll up and enjoy.

MAKES: 4 servings

PREPARATION TIME: 10 minutes / COOKING TIME: 6 minutes

Nutrients per serving: 10.3 g protein, 9.8 g total fat (2.6 g saturated, 8 mg cholesterol), 46.7 g carbohydrates, 3.3 mg iron, 58 mg calcium, 514 mg sodium, 7.4 g fibre, 306 calories

Excellent source of vitamin A and folic acid.
Good source of iron.
High amount of dietary fibre.

beta carotene

vitamin C

Orange
and Yellow
fruits and veggies

Intensely coloured fruits and vegetables such as carrots, sweet potatoes, peppers, mangoes and papaya get their hue from beta carotene, an antioxidant that neutralizes free radicals — unstable toxic molecules that jet around our body damaging cells and which can lead to diseases such as cancer, heart disease and stroke.

fibre

Squash and Fennel Soup

Fennel's mild anise flavour seasons squash so this soup tastes rich without any added cream. We got the idea from Toronto's Adega Restaurant.

1	fennel bulb	1
1	onion	1
1	large celery stalk	1
1	small squash or 14-oz (400-g) pkg frozen puréed squash	1
1 tbsp	butter	15 mL
2	(10-oz/284-mL) cans condensed chicken broth, preferably salt-reduced, mixed with 2 cups (500 mL) water or 4½ cups (1.12 L) chicken or vegetable bouillon	2
½ tsp	salt (optional)	2 mL

1. Cut fronds (feathery leaves) from fennel and save for garnish. Cut out small core from bulb. Thickly slice bulb and white parts of fronds. Coarsely chop onion and celery. Peel (see Tip, below), seed and cut fresh squash into cubes.

2. Heat butter in a large saucepan over medium heat. Add onion and celery. Cook until onion has softened, about 5 minutes. Stir in fennel, squash and enough undiluted broth and water to cover vegetables. Bring to a boil. Then reduce heat, cover and simmer until vegetables are very tender, from 15 to 30 minutes.

3. Purée vegetables in several batches in a food processor. Return to saucepan. Stir in remaining liquid. Heat, stirring often, until hot. Add salt, if needed. Ladle soup into bowls, then float a small piece of frond on top. Soup will keep well, covered and refrigerated, for 3 days or freeze.

MAKES: 7 cups (1.75 L)

PREPARATION TIME: 30 minutes / COOKING TIME: 25 minutes

TIP: For easy peeling, place whole unpeeled squash — acorn or butternut are ideal varieties — in a microwave. Cook on high for 2 minutes. Slice off peel. Or if slicing is still difficult, microwave another 2 minutes.

Nutrients per cup (250 mL): 2 g protein, 1.9 g total fat (1.1 g saturated, 5 mg cholesterol), 10.6 g carbohydrates, 0.5 mg iron, 38 mg calcium, 535 mg sodium, 2.5 g fibre, 59 calories

Moderate amount of dietary fibre.

Ethereal Sweet Potato and Mango Soup

A naturally flavoured sweet potato and mango creation that we tasted at the 7 West Café on Charles Street in Toronto inspired this lovely soup.

1	large red or white Spanish onion	1
2 tsp	olive oil	10 mL
1 tsp	each of ground cumin and curry powder	5 mL
4	large sweet potatoes, about 2 lbs (1 kg)	4
3	(10-oz/284-mL) cans condensed chicken broth	3
4 cups	water	1 L
2	carrots	2
2	celery stalks, including leaves	2
2	very ripe mangoes, about 3 cups (750 mL) chunks	2

1. Coarsely chop onion. Heat oil in a large saucepan over medium-low heat. Add onion. Sprinkle with cumin and curry. Stir often until soft, about 5 minutes. Peel potatoes and cut each into 8 pieces. Add to softened onions with undiluted broth and water. Cover and bring to a boil over high heat. Slice carrots and celery into ½-inch (1-cm) pieces and add to soup. When boiling, decrease heat and boil gently, covered, until vegetables are very soft, from 25 to 35 minutes.

2. While vegetables cook, peel mangoes and slice flesh from around stone. When potatoes and carrots are very soft, remove soup from heat. Pour most of liquid out into a bowl. Working in batches, place a portion of cooked vegetables in a blender or food processor fitted with a metal blade along with enough of liquid to make puréeing possible. Liquefy, using an on-and-off motion, until mixture is smooth. Stop and scrape down sides occasionally. Add mango to last batch of vegetables. Return puréed vegetables and fruit to broth.

3. Taste soup and add salt and pepper, if you like. Thin, if necessary, with hot water. Serve right away or refrigerate for up to 3 days or freeze. This soup is best served piping hot or very cold with a swirl of yogurt or sour cream in centre and a sprinkle of toasted cumin seeds and coriander leaves on top.

MAKES: 14 cups (3.5 L)

PREPARATION TIME: 20 minutes / COOKING TIME: 30 minutes

Nutrients per cup (250 mL): 4.4 g protein, 1.6 g total fat (0.3 g saturated, 1 mg cholesterol), 22.1 g carbohydrates, 0.8 mg iron, 35 mg calcium, 426 sodium, 3 g fibre, 115 calories

Excellent source of vitamin A.
Good source of vitamin C.
Moderate amount of dietary fibre.

Roasted Garlic-Ginger Sweet Potato Soup

This is a good entertaining soup as it can easily be made in advance — even weeks ahead and frozen — without any flavour loss.

6	large sweet potatoes	6
1 tbsp	vegetable oil	15 mL
½	head garlic, about 5 unpeeled cloves	½
2 to 3	slices ginger	2 to 3
6 cups	chicken broth or bouillon	1.5 L
1 to 2 cups	water	250 to 500 mL

1. Preheat oven to 350°F (180°C). Slice potatoes in half lengthwise. Rub cut surfaces with oil and place cut-side down on a baking sheet. Scatter unpeeled garlic cloves and peeled ginger slices in centre of pan. Bake, uncovered, in centre of oven until potatoes are very soft, from 45 to 60 minutes.

2. Then scoop half the potato pulp from skins and place in a food processor. Squeeze garlic cloves from peel right into processor. Add ginger. Whirl, adding broth as needed to produce a purée. Turn purée into a large saucepan. Then purée remaining potato pulp. Stir in remaining broth and water, 1 cup (250 mL) at a time, until as thick as you like. Add to saucepan. Heat over medium-low, stirring frequently to prevent scorching, until hot. Serve with dollops of sour cream. Soup will keep well, covered and refrigerated, up to 3 days.

MAKES: 10 cups (2.5 L)

PREPARATION TIME: 25 minutes / BAKING TIME: 45 minutes

Nutrients per cup (250 mL): 6.1 g protein, 2.4 g total fat (0.4 g saturated, 0 mg cholesterol), 43.2 g carbohydrates, 1.1 mg iron, 58 mg calcium, 485 sodium, 5.2 g fibre, 217 calories

Excellent source of vitamins A, C and B6.
Good source of folic acid.
High amount of dietary fibre.

Chilled Cantaloupe and Berry Soup

This soup, packed with vitamin C-rich strawberries and cantaloupe and flavoured with a wisp of fresh ginger, is fabulous to begin a weekend lunch or brunch party. While it works with light sour cream, you'll get a better texture with regular.

2	medium-size very ripe cantaloupes, about 2 lbs (1 kg) each	2
½ to 1 cup	sour cream	125 to 250 mL
½ cup	thickly sliced strawberries	125 mL
1 tsp	grated fresh ginger or 1 tbsp (15 mL) finely chopped ginger	5 mL
1 to 2 tsp	freshly squeezed lime juice	5 to 10 mL
	fresh mint leaves (optional)	
	sliced strawberries (optional)	

1. Cut cantaloupes in half. Using a spoon, remove and discard seeds. Cut into wedges, slice off peel, then cut into large chunks. You should have about 7 cups (1.75 L).

2. Place cantaloupe chunks, ½ cup (125 mL) sour cream, strawberries, ginger and 1 teaspoon (5 mL) lime juice in bowl of a food processor or blender. Work in batches if necessary. Blend until smooth. Taste and whisk in additional sour cream and remaining lime juice, as needed.

3. Refrigerate at least until cold, from 2 to 4 hours or up to 2 days. Chill soup bowls in the freezer or the refrigerator. Ladle soup into chilled bowls, then garnish with mint leaves and strawberry slices, if you like.

MAKES: 4 cups (1 L)

PREPARATION TIME: 10 minutes / REFRIGERATION TIME: 2 hours

Nutrients per cup (250 mL): 3.4 g protein, 4.9 g total fat (2.5 g saturated, 11 mg cholesterol), 25.3 g carbohydrates, 0.7 mg iron, 63 mg calcium, 37 mg sodium, 2.3 g fibre, 145 calories

Excellent source of vitamins A and C. **Good source of** vitamin B6 and folic acid.
Moderate amount of dietary fibre.

Roasted Pepper Bouillabaisse

The heady flavour of roasted red pepper adds new dimension to this saffron-laced fish soup.

4	sweet red peppers	4
	or 12-oz (340-g) jar roasted red peppers	
4	canned or 2 peeled fresh tomatoes	4
2	(10-oz/284 mL) cans condensed chicken broth	2
1 cup	water	250 mL
½ cup	white wine	125 mL
2	minced garlic cloves	2
¼ tsp	each of hot red chili flakes, basil and salt	1 mL
¼ tsp	saffron threads	1 mL
1	leek	1
1 lb	firm-fleshed fish such as monkfish or catfish	500 g
1 tsp	granulated sugar (optional)	5 mL
	chopped fresh coriander or basil (optional)	

1. If using fresh peppers, preheat oven to 450°F (230°C). Place peppers on a foil-lined baking sheet. Roast, until at least half of skin is charred, about 20 minutes. Remove from oven. Pull edges of foil over peppers and enclose so they will steam, making skins easier to peel. When cool, peel skin and discard. Core and seed. Meanwhile, finely chop tomatoes. Combine tomatoes with juice, undiluted broth, water, wine, garlic and seasonings in a large wide saucepan. Crush saffron threads between your fingers and add. Cover and bring to a boil over high heat.

2. Meanwhile, slice tough green leaves and root end from leek and discard. Slice leek lengthwise. Wash sand from between leaves under cold running water. Thinly slice crosswise. Stir into soup. Cover, reduce heat to low. Simmer 20 minutes, stirring often to develop flavours.

3. As soon as peppers are peeled, coarsely chop and add to soup. If using a jar of peppers, drain well, chop and add. After soup has simmered 20 minutes, slice fish into bite-size pieces and add. Cover and cook just until fish flakes, from 6 to 8 minutes. Taste and add sugar, if needed. Serve in heated bowls sprinkled with chopped fresh coriander or basil.

MAKES: 7 cups (1.75 L)

PREPARATION TIME: 30 minutes / COOKING TIME: 30 minutes

Nutrients per cup (250 mL): 17.7 g protein, 3.7 g total fat (1 g saturated, 26 mg cholesterol), 8.3 g carbohydrates, 1.6 mg iron, 26 mg calcium, 688 mg sodium, 1.8 g fibre, 141 calories

Excellent source of vitamins A and C. **Good source of** vitamin B6 and folic acid.
High amount of dietary fibre.

Carrots and Celery in a Spicy Sauce Dressing

Don't underestimate the power of celery just because it's 90 percent water. Long before it was enjoyed as a food it was grown as a medicinal plant, which Asian medicine has used for ages. It lowers blood pressure and is said to have a calming effect. However, celery is prone to nitrates used in fertilizers, so look for organic celery. This exciting side dish — served hot, cold or at room temperature — will liven up chicken, grilled fish or steak.

¼ cup	seasoned rice vinegar	50 mL
1 tbsp	granulated sugar	15 mL
1 tsp	salt	5 mL
1	bunch celery, about 1¾ lbs (875 g)	1
4	carrots, about 1 lb (500 g)	4
2 tbsp	sesame oil	30 mL
¼ tsp	hot red chili flakes	1 mL
3 tbsp	thinly sliced green onions	45 mL
1 tbsp	rice wine or sake	15 mL

1. In a small bowl, stir rice vinegar with sugar and salt. Set aside. Rinse celery stalks. Using a vegetable peeler, peel away any tough outer skin on celery and peel carrots. Cut root ends and leafy tops from both. Slice celery diagonally into thin pieces. Halve carrots lengthwise, then slice into thin half moons.

2. Heat oil in a large frying pan over medium heat. As soon as it is hot, add carrots. Cook, partially covered and stirring often, to slightly soften carrots, about 5 minutes. Stir in celery, chili flakes and onions. Stir often for 2 minutes. Increase heat to high. Add rice wine. Lightly toss for 2 minutes. Add rice vinegar mixture. Stir often until vegetables are just tender, from 1 to 2 minutes more. Serve right away or leave at room temperature for up to 1 hour. Covered and refrigerated, dish will keep well for 2 days.

MAKES: 6 servings

PREPARATION TIME: 15 minutes / COOKING TIME: 10 minutes

Nutrients per serving: 1.8 g protein, 4.8 g total fat (0.7 g saturated, 0 mg cholesterol), 17.8 g carbohydrates, 1 mg iron, 73 mg calcium, 887 mg sodium, 3.5 g fibre, 118 calories

Excellent source of vitamin A.
Good source of folic acid.
Moderate amount of dietary fibre.

Health Wonders

Phytochemicals

The power of the plant world is truly mind-boggling. The research doesn't stop coming. Eat your fruits and vegetables – the magic numbers as always are from five to nine servings – and health will be yours. A plant's chemistry or phytochemical (phyto is Greek for plant) has taught us much.

What are these mysterious phytochemicals? Well, they are not vitamins or minerals and they have no known nutritional value. So why bother, you ask? Because what they do have is the ability to influence disease, especially the biggies like cancer and heart disease. They work in many different ways and combinations. Don't be put off by the science-lab-sounding names, they'll soon be as familiar as cholesterol. Here's a roundup of the major players.

Carotenoids

Carotenoids are proven fighters of free radical scavengers that raid our bodies and damage healthy cell membranes and tissue. There are more than 500 different carotenoids, including beta carotene, lycopene, lutein and zeaxantin.

Beta carotene is the antioxidant plant pigment responsible for the vibrant oranges and yellows found in fruits and vegetables like cantaloupes and sweet potatoes. Spinach and other dark green vegetables are also high in beta carotene, but their colour is masked by green chlorophyll.

Lycopene, the red pigment in tomatoes, is also a potent carotenoid believed to fight cervical and prostate cancers.

Polyphenols

This is a huge class of phytochemicals and one that has received a lot of press because it contains the much-touted flavonoids, which are found in tea – both green and black – red grapes and red wine and are believed to have anti-cancer effects and heart benefits.

Allylic sulfides are also flavonoids and, true to their name, are responsible for the strong flavour and smell found in garlic, onions and shallots. They help lower blood pressure, reduce the risk of heart disease and may help the body rid itself of cancer-causing substances.

Anthocyanidins are another flavonoid, but in this case they act as a pigment and add colour to strawberries, raspberries and blueberries. They are a potent antioxidant that have anti-cancer properties and may also protect against heart disease.

Phytoestrogens

Phytoestrogens are plant compounds that have hormone-like effects on the body. They come in two varieties – isoflavones, which are also flavonoids (see Polyphenols, left), found in soybeans, and lignans found in flaxseeds, whole grains and fennel. Phytoestrogens are said to inhibit tumours and some studies have noticed a link between soy-rich diets and a lower risk of breast cancer and a decline in menopausal symptoms (see Flax Facts, page 101, and Soy and Menopause, page 115.)

Phytosterols

Phytosterols belong to the sterol family. Cholesterol is also a member. They are both fat compounds, but phytosterols come from the plant world, while dietary cholesterol comes from animal products. However, unlike dietary cholesterol, phytosterols have health benefits. They have been shown to reduce the levels of bad cholesterol (LDL) without affecting the good cholesterol (HDL) and may protect against colon and other cancers. They are found in plants that contain fat such as peanuts, soybeans, sesame and sunflower seeds and sesame and sunflower oils.

Saponins

Saponins get their name from the soapwort plant, whose root was used as a soap. Plants containing saponins, such as chickpeas and soybeans, tend to have a soapy texture and foam in water. Saponins have anti-cancer effects (see Phytoestrogens, above).

Gall Bladder Disease and Vitamin C

Low levels of vitamin C can up your odds of developing gall bladder disease, according to a study published in the *Archives of Internal Medicine*. Epidemiologists examining 13,130 people found that women who had low levels of vitamin C in their blood had an 8 percent higher risk of the disease and a 5 percent higher risk of asymptomatic gallstones. But women who took vitamin supplements had a 34 percent lower prevalence of gall bladder disease. In men, there was no relationship between supplements and the condition. The researchers recommended increased consumption of fruit and vegetables and a vitamin C supplement.

Magnificent Mango Salad

Magnificent, indeed! Mango is the best fruit source of beta carotene and a good source of soluble fibre, known to keep blood cholesterol low. It is also one of the few good fruit sources of vitamin E. This Asian-inspired salad is not only healthy and refreshing, it's a visual winner too!

1	large ripe lime	1
1 tbsp	fish sauce	15 mL
1 tbsp	granulated sugar	15 mL
½ tsp	hot red chili flakes	2 mL
2	ripe mangoes, about 3 cups (750 mL) large chunks	2
2	red peppers	2
½	small red onion	½
½ cup	coarsely chopped fresh mint	125 mL
½ cup	coarsely chopped coriander leaves	125 mL
	salt (optional)	
2 tbsp	coarsely chopped toasted peanuts (optional)	30 mL

1. Squeeze juice from lime and place 2 tablespoons (30 mL) in a large bowl. Stir in fish sauce, sugar and chili flakes until sugar is dissolved.

2. Peel mangoes, slice pulp from stone, then cut into bite-size julienne strips. Slice peppers into bite-size julienne strips. Combine mangoes and red pepper in a bowl. Finely chop onion and add along with mint and half of coriander. Taste and add more lime juice or a little salt, if you like.

3. Salad is best if it sits at room temperature for 1 hour. Sprinkle salad with remaining coriander and peanuts, if using. Serve right away or refrigerate. Salad can be refrigerated for up to 1 day but mint will darken, so add just before serving.

MAKES: 4 to 6 servings
PREPARATION TIME: 20 minutes / STANDING TIME: 1 hour

Nutrients per serving: 1.4 g protein, 0.4 total fat (0.1 g saturated, 0 mg cholesterol), 22.7 g carbohydrates, 0.6 mg iron, 29 mg calcium, 237 mg sodium, 3 g fibre, 90 calories

Excellent source of vitamins A and C.
Moderate amount of dietary fibre.

Harvest Beet Salad with Tangerines and Celeriac

Beets, oranges and fresh dill are one of our favourite fall salad combinations. Serve it after the entrée as a mini-course.

¼ cup	toasted pecan halves	50 mL
8 cups	mixed salad greens, about ½ lb (250 g)	2 L
1 cup	peeled julienned celeriac	250 mL
4	cooked peeled beets or 14-oz (398-mL) can beets	4
4	tangerines, clementines or oranges	4
¼ cup	olive oil	50 mL
¼ cup	cider vinegar	50 mL
1 tsp	Dijon mustard	5 mL
1 tsp	liquid honey	5 mL
½ tsp	each of salt and freshly ground black pepper	2 mL
2 tbsp	chopped fresh dill or ½ tsp (2 mL) dried dillweed	30 mL

1. To toast nuts, spread out evenly on a baking sheet. Place in preheated 325°F (160°C) oven until fragrant and golden, about 10 minutes. Meanwhile, wash and dry greens. Place in a salad bowl. Peel and julienne celeriac. If making ahead, place celeriac on top of greens and cover with a damp paper towel. Refrigerate for up to 4 hours.

2. Thinly slice beets and set aside. Finely grate enough peel from tangerines to measure 2 teaspoons (10 mL). Peel tangerines and remove any pith. Separate into sections. If using oranges, slice into rounds. Tangerines and beets can be left at room temperature separately for several hours or refrigerated separately for at least 1 day.

3. In a small bowl, whisk oil with peel, vinegar, mustard, honey, salt and pepper. Stir in dill. If making ahead, leave at room temperature for up to 1 day or refrigerate up to 2 days. Just before serving, toss greens, celeriac and tangerines with dressing. Scatter beets and nuts over top.

MAKES: 6 to 8 servings

PREPARATION TIME: 20 minutes / TOASTING TIME: 10 minutes

Nutrients per serving: 2.7 g protein, 9.4 g total fat (1.1 g saturated, 0 mg cholesterol), 17.2 g carbohydrates, 1.2 mg iron, 67 mg calcium, 209 mg sodium, 3.4 g fibre, 153 calories

Excellent source of vitamin C and folic acid.
Moderate amount of dietary fibre.

Spicy Party Couscous

With very little work and in an incredibly short period of time, you can create a vegetable-laced couscous — beautiful enough to be the centrepiece of a buffet or the perfect companion to roast chicken. Besides beta carotene from the carrots and sweet peppers, this recipe contains lots of ginger, reputed to prevent motion sickness.

2	(10-oz/284-mL) cans condensed chicken broth	2
1	large onion, preferably red, coarsely chopped	1
4	large minced garlic cloves or 1 tbsp (15 mL) bottled minced garlic	4
¼ cup	finely chopped fresh ginger or 1 tbsp (15 mL) bottled minced ginger	50 mL
2 tsp	ground cumin	10 mL
1 tsp	cinnamon	5 mL
¼ tsp	hot red chili flakes or cayenne pepper	1 mL
1-lb	bag baby carrots	454-g
½ cup	water	125 mL
2 tbsp	butter	30 mL
2	sweet peppers, preferably 1 red and 1 green, chopped	2
¼ to ½ cup	raisins	50 to 125 mL
2 cups	couscous	500 mL

1. In a large wide saucepan, bring undiluted chicken broth, onion, garlic, ginger, cumin, cinnamon and chili flakes to a boil. Cover and cook over medium heat, stirring often, for 5 minutes.

2. Stir in carrots and continue cooking, covered, until almost tender, about 8 minutes. Then add water, butter, peppers and raisins. Bring to a boil. Stir in couscous and remove from heat. Let sit, covered, for 5 minutes. Fluff with a fork. Wonderful hot or at room temperature.

MAKES: 8 cups (2 L)
PREPARATION TIME: 15 minutes / COOKING TIME: 20 minutes

Nutrients per cup (250 mL): 11.1 g protein, 4.4 g total fat (2.1 g saturated, 9 mg cholesterol), 54.2 g carbohydrates, 2.1 mg iron, 62 mg calcium, 549 mg sodium, 5.1 g fibre, 297 calories

Excellent source of vitamins A and C. **Good source of** vitamin B6 and folic acid.
High amount of dietary fibre.

Our Favourite Roasted Sweet Potato Wedges

Delicious healthy sweet potatoes — the copper-skinned tubers with vivid orange flesh — are increasingly brightening up fall meals. These oven-baked sweet potato chili fries make a spicy nutritious snack or side dish.

3	sweet potatoes	3
1 tbsp	olive oil	15 mL
1 tbsp	brown sugar	15 mL
½ tsp	chili powder	2 mL
¼ tsp	salt	1 mL
¼ tsp	cayenne pepper	1 mL

1. Preheat oven to 400°F (200°C). Peel potatoes and cut into 1-inch (2.5-cm) wedges. In a large bowl, toss with oil. Sprinkle with remaining ingredients and stir until evenly coated.

2. Lightly oil a roasting pan or baking dish or 2 pans large enough to hold potatoes without crowding. Spread wedges out on pans. Roast potatoes in oven, stirring every 10 minutes, until tender and browned, about 35 minutes.

MAKES: 4 servings
PREPARATION TIME: 10 minutes / ROASTING TIME: 35 minutes

Nutrients per serving: 3.2 g protein, 3.7 g total fat (0.5 g saturated, 0 mg cholesterol), 48.1 g carbohydrates, 1 mg iron, 55 mg calcium, 166 mg sodium, 5.6 fibre, 233 calories

Excellent source of vitamins A and C. **Good source of** vitamin B6 and folic acid.
High amount of dietary fibre.

New-Style Stuffed Peppers

We've used low-fat ground chicken here which contains less than 10 percent fat so there's only 158 calories per pepper half.

½ lb	ground chicken or turkey	250 g
1 tsp	ground cumin	5 mL
¼ tsp	salt	1 mL
¼ tsp	hot red chili flakes (optional)	1 mL
3	medium-size sweet peppers, preferably a mix of colours	3
19-oz	can tomatoes, including juice	540-mL
¾ cup	uncooked instant or quick-cooking rice	175 mL
½ cup	kernel corn, frozen or canned	125 mL
2	green onions, sliced	2

1. Preheat oven to 375°F (190°C). Crumble chicken into a large non-stick frying pan over medium heat. Sprinkle with seasonings. Cook, working with a fork to keep chicken crumbly, until it loses its pink colour, from 6 to 8 minutes.

2. Meanwhile, slice peppers in half, lengthwise through stem. Remove stem and seeds. Drain juice from tomatoes into a measuring cup. Add water to tomato juice to bring level to ¾ cup (175 mL).

3. Place tomatoes in large mixing bowl. Using a fork, break up tomatoes. Add tomato juice to bowl. Stir in cooked chicken, uncooked rice, corn and green onions.

4. Spoon mixture into pepper halves, mounding in centres. Arrange filled pepper halves in an ungreased 9x13-inch (3-L) baking dish. Cover tightly with a tent of foil and bake in centre of oven until peppers are tender when pierced with a fork and rice is tender, from 35 to 40 minutes.

MAKES: 6 halves for 3 servings

PREPARATION TIME: 20 minutes / COOKING TIME: 6 minutes / BAKING TIME: 35 minutes

Nutrients per 2 pepper halves: 19.9 g protein, 8.6 g total fat (2.3 g saturated, 59 mg cholesterol), 41.6 g carbohydrates, 3.3 mg iron, 81 mg calcium, 545 mg sodium, 5.4 g fibre, 316 calories

Excellent source of vitamins A, C and B6.
Good source of folic acid.
High amount of dietary fibre.

Barbecued Squash
with Seared Maple Butter

Since squash takes almost an hour to grill, unless you are barbecuing something large, such as a turkey, it's best to precook the squash in the microwave or conventional oven before finishing on the grill.

2	medium-size acorn squash, about 4½ inches (11 cm) in diameter	2
2 tbsp	butter, at room temperature	30 mL
2 tbsp	maple syrup or liquid honey	30 mL
½ tsp	cinnamon	2 mL
¼ tsp	each of allspice and ground ginger	1 mL
pinch	salt	pinch
	chopped chives and rosemary sprigs (optional)	

1. To make squash easy to slice, microwave whole on high power for 3 minutes. Remove, slice in half and scoop out seeds. Return halves to microwave, cut-side down. Cook, on high power until almost fork-tender, from 10 to 16 minutes, depending on size and ripeness. Place cut-side down on a plate until ready to barbecue. Or refrigerate for up to 2 days if not barbecuing right away.

2. Oil grill and preheat barbecue to medium-high. Lightly oil cut sides of squash and place cut-side down on grill. Barbecue with lid down until grill marks form, from 5 to 8 minutes.

3. Meanwhile, stir butter with maple syrup and spices and salt. Turn squash and place an equal amount of maple mixture in centre of each half. Spread or brush over all squash flesh. Continue to barbecue with lid closed until squash is glazed, up to 20 minutes. Serve squash halved or in thick rounds. Sprinkle with chives and garnish halves with 2 rosemary sprigs inserted into centre of squash, if you wish.

Barbecue or Oven: Wrap squash halves in heavy foil, then barbecue with lid down, turning often, until almost fork-tender, about 40 minutes. Remove foil. Glaze as above. Or bake squash halves cut-side down on a baking sheet at 350°F (180°C) until almost fork-tender, about 40 minutes. Glaze as above on barbecue or broil on centre rack until glazed, about 6 minutes.

MAKES: 4 servings

PREPARATION TIME: 2 minutes / MICROWAVING TIME: 13 minutes / GRILLING TIME: 25 minutes

---

Nutrients per half: 1.9 g protein, 6 g total fat (3.6 g saturated, 16 mg cholesterol), 29.6 g carbohydrates, 1.7 mg iron, 82 mg calcium, 66 mg sodium, 5.4 g fibre, 165 calories

Excellent source of magnesium.
Good source of vitamin B6.
High amount of dietary fibre.

Minted Melon Salsa

Mint is the ideal summer herb. It adds a touch of elegance to this pretty, low-cal, almost no-fat salsa.

1	small cantaloupe	1
½	English cucumber, diced	½
¼ cup	finely chopped fresh mint	50 mL
2 tbsp	freshly squeezed lime juice	30 mL
1 tbsp	liquid honey	15 mL

1. Chop cantaloupe pulp fairly small and place in a medium-size bowl. Stir with cucumber and mint. Stir lime juice with honey until evenly mixed. Then stir into cantaloupe mixture until evenly coated. Use right away or refrigerate for up to 1 day. Serve over grilled chicken, veal chops or fish steaks.

MAKES: 2 cups (500 mL)

PREPARATION TIME: 10 minutes

Nutrients per ¼ cup (50 mL): 0.7 g protein, 0.2 g total fat (0 g saturated, 0 mg cholesterol), 7.5 g carbohydrates, 0.2 mg iron, 12 mg calcium, 6 mg sodium, 0.7 g fibre, 30 calories

Good source of vitamins A and C.

Health Wonders

Pigment Power

Bright-coloured mangoes and carrots, as well as other intensely hued produce, such as red peppers and cantaloupe, are bursting with the antioxidants vitamin C and beta carotene, which the body converts to vitamin A.

One study showed men with the lowest levels of beta carotene in their blood were at the greatest risk of developing prostate cancer.

Orange and yellow fruit and veggies are storehouses of phytochemicals that may provide some protection against various hormone-related cancers; folic acid, which can help prevent birth defects; and fibre, which may reduce the risk of some cancers such as colon cancer.

Papaya

Half a medium papaya contains about 60 calories. It's loaded with nutrients including vitamin C, calcium, small amounts of the B vitamins, iron and zinc. It is also an excellent source of potassium. Papayas are actually large berries, good eaten fresh or cooked, wonderful in a fruit salad or salsa or as an accompaniment to seafood and chicken.

Mangoes

Juicy, sweet mangoes are high in beta carotene, vitamin C and fibre, and a whole mango has only 135 calories. Slice over your breakfast cereal, make a fresh mango salad for lunch, serve a mango salsa with fish or chicken or enjoy alone as a sweet snack.

Cantaloupe

Cantaloupe is one of the most nutritionally well-rounded fruits. Half a melon, at about 90 calories, contains more than your daily requirement of vitamin C, is loaded with beta carotene, folic acid and potassium and is virtually fat-free.

Veggies and Calcium

Move over, calcium. Fruit and vegetables can also keep women's bones strong, says a study in the *American Journal of Clinical Nutrition*. British nutritionists examined the eating habits of 62 women ages 45 to 55 and scanned their bones for density. Women whose diets included a lot of fruit and vegetables had a higher bone mass and experienced less bone loss. Fruit and vegetables contain bone-boosting nutrients such as potassium, which slows the excretion of calcium, and vitamin C and magnesium, which seem to help bone formation.

Tropical Mango-Papaya Salsa

Keep this salsa in mind to dress up anything that comes off the barbecue.

1	large ripe papaya	1
1	ripe mango, about 1½ cups (375 mL) large chunks	1
1	ripe avocado	1
1 tbsp	seeded and finely chopped fresh jalapeño	15 mL
3 tbsp	freshly squeezed lime juice	45 mL
⅓ cup	finely chopped fresh coriander	75 mL
	salt (optional)	

1. Peel and seed papaya, mango and avocado. Dice into ¼-inch (0.5-cm) pieces. Stir in a bowl along with remaining ingredients. Taste and add salt, if needed.

2. Use immediately or cover and refrigerate for up to 1 day. The avocado may darken as it sits. This salsa is great served with grilled lamb kabobs, shrimp, chicken or swordfish steaks.

MAKES: 2 cups (500 mL)

PREPARATION TIME: 10 minutes

Nutrients ¼ cup (50 mL): 0.8 g protein, 4 g total fat (0.6 g saturated, 0 mg cholesterol), 8.7 g carbohydrates, 0.4 mg iron, 13 mg calcium, 4 mg sodium, 1.5 g fibre, 67 calories

Good source of vitamins A and C.

Papaya-Coriander Salsa

Papaya is at the top when it comes to vitamin C. The tropical fruit even beats out an 8-oz (250-mL) glass of orange juice — 188 mg for a medium papaya to 124 mg for the juice. Spoon over any grilled fish or chicken and you'll add an instant touch of the tropics.

1	large ripe papaya	1
3 tbsp	chopped fresh coriander	45 mL
2	green onions, chopped	2
1 tbsp	seeded and finely chopped fresh jalapeño	15 mL
1 tsp	freshly squeezed lime juice	5 mL
½ tsp	granulated sugar	2 mL
pinch	salt (optional)	pinch

1. Peel and seed papaya. Dice into ¼-inch (0.5-cm) pieces. In a medium-size bowl, gently mix papaya with remaining ingredients. Taste and add salt, if needed.

2. Serve immediately or cover and refrigerate for up to 1 day. This salsa is delicious with grilled chicken, fish or served over scrambled eggs with English muffins.

MAKES: 2 cups (500 mL)

PREPARATION TIME: 10 minutes

Nutrients per ¼ cup (50 mL) : 0.4 g protein, 0.1 g total fat (0 g saturated, 0 mg cholesterol), 5.5 g carbohydrates, 0.1 mg iron, 16 mg calcium, 3 mg sodium, 1 g fibre, 22 calories

Excellent source of vitamin C.

omega-3 fatty

protein

Salmon
and other
heart-healthy fish

Salmon, as well as other cold-water fish such as mackerel, sardines, herring, fresh tuna and trout, is a big carrier of omega-3 fatty acids. These polyunsaturated fish oils may dramatically reduce the formation of blood clots which can lead to strokes and heart attacks, decrease cancer growth and may offer protection against inflammatory diseases such as arthritis. Just one portion of fish per week can help prevent heart attacks. These cold-water fish may even play a role in brain development and function (see Fish and Depression, page 91). It's also a great way to catch vitamin B, selenium and lots of protein with very little saturated fat.

Honey-Mustard Salmon Fillets

Rich in heart-healthy omega-3 fatty acids, luscious salmon fillets pair up with honey, mustard and zesty lemon peel for this sophisticated entrée.

1	lime	1
2 tsp	liquid honey	10 mL
1 tsp	Dijon or 1 tbsp (15 mL) honey mustard	5 mL
2	serving-size salmon fillets or salmon steaks, at least 1 inch (2.5 cm) thick	2

1. Preheat oven broiler or barbecue. Finely grate a little peel from lime, about ¼ tsp (1 mL). Stir with honey and mustard. Spread over surface of salmon but not on skin. Fish can be cooked right away or refrigerated for up to 2 hours.

2. When ready to cook, if broiling, line a baking sheet with foil for easy cleanup. Place coated steaks on a greased rack and place on foil-covered baking sheet. Or lightly oil foil and place coated steaks directly on foil. Then broil about 4 inches (10 cm) from element until sizzling, 10 minutes for fillets or 5 minutes each side for steaks. If barbecuing, place coated fish on an oiled grill on preheated barbecue. Barbecue for 5 to 6 minutes each side. Then squeeze lime juice over hot steaks. Great with mesclun greens.

MAKES: 2 servings

PREPARATION TIME: 5 minutes / GRILLING TIME: 10 minutes

Nutrients per serving: 29.6 g protein, 16.6 g total fat (3.3 g saturated, 84 mg cholesterol), 7.7 g carbohydrates, 0.5 mg iron, 26 mg calcium, 115 mg sodium, 0.1 g fibre, 302 calories

Excellent source of vitamins B_6 and B_{12}.
Good source of folic acid.

Seared Tuna Marengo

Simple yet sophisticated recipes are trademarks of John Bishop, owner of Bishop's, one of Vancouver's finest restaurants. This recipe is adapted from his award-winning book, Cooking at My House *(Douglas & McIntyre). We love that the black olive-infused tomato topping can be made a day ahead, leaving only searing the fish to do at the last minute.*

8	shiitake or 6 medium-size portobello mushrooms, stems removed	8
10	ripe plum tomatoes or 4 very ripe round tomatoes	10
1	large or 2 small jalapeño peppers (optional)	1
3 tbsp	olive oil, preferably full flavoured	45 mL
¼ tsp	salt	1 mL
½ cup	coarsely chopped pitted black olives, about 25	125 mL
4	(6-oz/180-g) tuna or halibut fillets, preferably 1½ inches (3.5 cm) thick	4
	olive or vegetable oil	
	salt and coarsely ground white or black pepper	

1. For sauce, slice mushrooms into ¼-inch (0.5-cm) thick bite-size strips. Core tomatoes, then slice in half. Squeeze out all juice and seeds and discard. Coarsely chop tomatoes. They should measure about 4 cups (1 L). Seed and finely chop jalapeño, if using. It should measure about 2 tablespoons (30 mL).

2. Heat oil in a large wide frying pan over medium-high heat. When piping hot, add mushrooms. Then sprinkle with salt. Stir-fry just until lightly browned, about 5 minutes. Stir in tomatoes, jalapeño and chopped olives. Cook over medium-high heat, uncovered and stirring often (especially near end of cooking), until most of liquid is evaporated and sauce is thick. This will take about 15 minutes. Add more salt, if needed. Use sauce right away or refrigerate, covered, for up to 2 days. Reheat over low heat or on medium power in microwave, stirring often.

3. To sear tuna, lightly coat a frying pan with oil. Place over medium-high heat. Lightly sprinkle tuna with salt and liberally with pepper. Place in hot pan. Sear from 2 to 4 minutes per side. (Two minutes per side will leave it very rare.) Place on warm dinner plates and top with sauce.

MAKES: 4 servings
PREPARATION TIME: 15 minutes / COOKING TIME: 25 minutes

Nutrients per serving: 45 g protein, 25.6 g total fat (4.3 g saturated, 65 mg cholesterol), 16.2 g carbohydrates, 5.7 mg iron, 47 mg calcium, 779 mg sodium, 6.3 g fibre, 463 calories

Excellent source of vitamins A, B6 and B12 and iron. **Good source of** vitamin C and folic acid. **Very high amount of** dietary fibre.

Fillets in Spiced Tomato Sauce

Don't be alarmed by the high amount of fat in this recipe — it's the good heart-healthy omega-3 kind and mackerel is packed with it. Hundreds of research papers conclude that at least one serving of an oily fish per week can help prevent heart attacks. The Heart and Stroke Foundation of Canada has been recommending including oily fish in your diet for years. This recipe would work wonderfully with your favourite fish fillets.

2	onions	2
3 tbsp	all-purpose flour	45 mL
¼ tsp	salt	0.5 mL
¼ tsp	freshly ground black pepper	0.5 mL
6	fresh mackerel fillets, about 6 oz (190 g) each	6
1 to 2 tbsp	olive oil	15 to 30 mL
3	minced garlic cloves	3
19-oz	can Mexican- or Italian-seasoned stewed tomatoes, including juice	540-g
¼ cup	sliced stuffed olives	50 mL
1 tbsp	drained capers	15 mL

1. Thinly slice onions and set aside. Measure flour into a shallow dish, such as a pie plate. Using a fork, stir in salt and pepper. Pat fish fillets dry. Coat both sides of fish in flour. Shake off excess flour. Heat 1 tablespoon (15 mL) oil in a large frying pan and add 3 fillets. Cook fillets until golden on both sides, from 2 to 4 minutes per side. Remove to a plate and cover to keep warm. Repeat with remaining fillets and oil if needed.

2. Add onions and garlic to pan. Cook, stirring often, to pick up any brown bits on bottom of pan, until onions are soft, about 4 minutes.

3. Stir in tomatoes, olives and capers. Return fish to pan. Spoon tomato sauce over top so fillets are submerged. Cover and simmer until fish flakes easily when tested with a fork, about 3 minutes. Serve with rice, noodles or potatoes. Spoon extra sauce over top.

MAKES: 6 servings

PREPARATION TIME: 20 minutes / COOKING TIME: 15 minutes

Nutrients per serving: 33.6 g protein, 27.1 g total fat (6 g saturated, 100 mg cholesterol), 11.6 g carbohydrates, 3.1 mg iron, 66 mg calcium, 577 mg sodium, 1.9 g fibre, 426 calories

Excellent source of vitamin B6.
Good source of iron.

Sardine Pâté

Sardines have one of the highest levels of omega-3 fatty acids. Here's an inexpensive way to get your omega-3s. It's easy enough to make up for a Saturday brunch. Serve it on toasted pitas.

4-oz	can sardines packed in water	106-g
1 tsp	Dijon mustard	5 mL
1 tsp	freshly squeezed lemon juice	5 mL
1	green onion, thinly sliced	1
½ tsp	freshly ground black pepper or hot pepper sauce	2 mL

1. Drain the fish well. Place in a bowl and mash with a fork. Stir in mustard, lemon juice and green onions. Then stir in pepper. Taste and add more Dijon or lemon juice, if you like. Use right away or refrigerate, covered, up to a day. Great served on toasted pita wedges.

MAKES: 2 servings

PREPARATION TIME: 5 minutes

Nutrients per serving: 9.3 g protein, 4.2 g total fat (1.2 g saturated, 25 mg cholesterol), 1.2 g carbohydrates, 1.4 mg iron, 182 mg calcium, 257 mg sodium, 0.2 g fibre, 78 calories

Excellent source of vitamin B_{12}.
Good source of calcium.

Miso-Hoisin Salmon

Healthy miso, a fermented soybean paste, gives a distinctive Japanese taste to the salmon steaks, and the preparation takes only 5 minutes.

1 tbsp	miso	15 mL
1 tbsp	hoisin sauce	15 mL
2	salmon steaks, at least 1 inch (2.5 cm) thick	2

1. Preheat oven to 450°F (230°C). Coat a foil-lined baking sheet with cooking spray or vegetable oil. In a small bowl, stir miso with hoisin sauce until evenly combined. Place salmon steaks on baking sheet and brush top with miso mixture. Bake salmon, uncovered and without turning, until it flakes easily, from 12 to 15 minutes.

MAKES: 2 servings

PREPARATION TIME: 5 minutes / BAKING TIME: 12 minutes

TIP: Miso is a mainstay of the Japanese diet. A fermented paste made from soybeans, miso is sold in the refrigerator section of some supermarkets, health food stores and Oriental markets. It's used in soups, sauces, marinades, dips and dressings. This easily digested paste has rich amounts of B vitamins and protein. Store miso in an airtight container. For more information on the health benefits of soy, see pages 111 and 115.

Nutrients per serving: 27.2 g protein, 15.3 g total fat (3.1 g saturated, 74 mg cholesterol), 5.9 g carbohydrates, 0.7 mg iron, 26 mg calcium, 514 mg sodium, 0.9 g fibre, 277 calories

Excellent source of vitamins B6 and B12.
Good source of folic acid.

Health Wonders

Colourful Salmon

The price of canned salmon is tied to its colour. Intensely red sockeye is the most expensive, while pale pink chum salmon is the best budget buy. Fortunately, while there's a big difference in price, there's little difference in nutrients.

All canned salmon packs an energy wallop. Half a can delivers 20 g protein, 13 g fat and about 150 calories. And if you eat it with the bones you'll get calcium.

The fat in canned salmon, and in all salmon, is rich in heart-healthy omega-3 fatty acids.

When choosing canned tuna, pick albacore tuna, which is usually marked "white" on the label. It tends to contain more omega-3s than other types, but when it comes to tuna, fresh is best.

Other Good News

Salmon has one of the highest amounts of omega-3 fatty acids than other popular fish and is also consistently lower priced. Plus, a 4-oz (120-g) portion of cooked salmon contains, on average, just 215 calories.

If You Knew Sushi

Many people are queasy about eating raw fish and it appears they may be on to something. Mackerel, salmon and herring are often host to the parasite anisakis/pseudoterranova, which can cause stomach pain if ingested.

The parasite doesn't pose a problem if fish has been frozen at –4°F (–20°C) for 24 to 48 hours, or if the fish is tuna.

Before you give up sushi, keep in mind that only 50 cases of ingestion of the parasite have been reported in the United States and one in Canada.

Maple-Ginger Salmon

We've married pure maple syrup with fresh ginger and lime for a sophisticated taste with little effort.

¼ cup	maple syrup	50 mL
2-inch	piece fresh ginger or 2 tbsp (30 mL) bottled minced ginger	5-cm
1	lime	1
1 tsp	sesame oil, preferably dark, or 1 tbsp (15 mL) olive or vegetable oil	5 mL
4	salmon steaks, at least 1 inch (2.5 cm) thick	4

1. Preheat oven broiler or barbecue and oil barbecue grill. Pour maple syrup into a small bowl. Finely mince or grate 2 tablespoons (30 mL) ginger and add to maple syrup. Squeeze juice from half a lime, about 1 tablespoon (15 mL). Stir juice and oil into maple mixture.

2. Generously brush salmon with maple mixture. Place on hot grill on a foil-lined baking sheet. Barbecue or broil about 3 inches (7.5 cm) from the element, brushing often with maple mixture and turning once, until fish is cooked as you like, from 5 to 6 minutes per side. For extra zing, squeeze juice from remaining half of lime over top of hot steaks. Serve right away with a mixture of wild and white rice and long thin green beans.

MAKES: 4 servings

PREPARATION TIME: 10 minutes / GRILLING TIME: 10 minutes

Nutrients per serving: 34.9 g protein, 20.3 g total fat (4.1 g saturated, 99 mg cholesterol), 12 g carbohydrates, 0.8 mg iron, 36 mg calcium, 99 mg sodium, 0.3 g fibre, 378 calories

Excellent source of vitamins B_6 and B_{12}.
Good source of folic acid.

Roasted Teriyaki Party Salmon

A special entrée doesn't get any easier to make than this flavourful salmon. We used a whole piece of salmon. Ask your fish merchant to skin it for you.

1	piece of whole salmon, skin removed, about 4 lbs (2 kg)	1
2 tbsp	sesame oil, preferably dark	30 mL
2 tbsp	teriyaki sauce	30 mL
2 tbsp	sesame seeds	30 mL

1. Preheat oven to 425°F (220°C). Line a large baking sheet with foil and coat with cooking spray. Rinse salmon under cold water. Pat dry. Place on baking sheet. Whisk oil with teriyaki. Brush inside and out with mixture. Spread half of seeds in cavity. Sprinkle remaining seeds over top.

2. Roast, uncovered, in centre of preheated oven for 10 minutes per inch (2.5 cm) of thickness at the fish's thickest part or until a knife point inserted into centre of salmon feels warm. Most whole salmon will be about 3 inches (7.5 cm) thick and will need about 30 minutes. Cut into serving pieces. Refrigerate any leftover salmon and serve cold the next day.

MAKES: 8 servings

PREPARATION TIME: 15 minutes / ROASTING TIME: 30 minutes

Nutrients per serving: 35.5 g protein, 24 g total fat (4.6 g saturated, 99 mg cholesterol), 0.9 g carbohydrates, 0.8 mg iron, 28 mg calcium, 269 mg sodium, 0.1 g fibre, 370 calories

Excellent source of vitamins B6 and B12 and folic acid.

Honey-Lime Glazed Salmon

A glistening side of salmon, flecked with bits of lime peel, makes a spectacular easy entertaining entrée. In the summer, make ahead, refrigerate and serve cold.

1	large or 2 small limes	1
1 tbsp	liquid honey	15 mL
1½ tsp	dark sesame oil	7 mL
1	boneless salmon fillet, about 4 lbs (2 kg)	1
¼ tsp	salt	0.5 mL

1. Preheat oven to 450°F (230°C). Finely grate peel from lime and squeeze out 2 tablespoons (30 mL) juice. Stir juice with peel, honey and oil.

2. Measure thickest part of salmon. Line a baking sheet with foil. Place fish, skin-side down, on ungreased foil. Brush salmon with some of lime mixture. Sprinkle with salt. Bake, uncovered, basting every 5 minutes with remaining sauce, for about 10 minutes per inch (2.5 cm) of thickness or until fish flakes easily with a fork. A 4-lb (2-kg), 2-inch (5-cm) thick side of salmon will need from 18 to 20 minutes. When fish is done, immediately transfer to a platter, leaving skin on foil. Serve right away or refrigerate until cold, at least 2 hours or for up to 1 day.

MAKES: 8 to 10 servings
PREPARATION TIME: 10 minutes / ROASTING TIME: 20 minutes

Nutrients per serving: 28.9 g protein, 16.8 g total fat (3.4 g saturated, 82 mg cholesterol), 2 g carbohydrates, 0.5 mg iron, 20 mg calcium, 137 mg sodium, 0 g fibre, 282 calories

Excellent source of vitamins B_6 and B_{12}.
Good source of folic acid.

Lemon Gremolada Fish

In many Mediterranean cuisines, the mixture of citrus peel, parsley and garlic is called gremolada and is used for a fresh flavour boost for long-simmered or braised dishes, such as osso buco. Here, fish steaks are marinated in gremolada before barbecuing.

1	large lemon	1
1	large orange	1
6	minced garlic cloves	6
½ cup	finely chopped fresh parsley or coriander or a mixture of both	125 mL
½ tsp	salt	2 mL
¼ cup	olive oil	50 mL
2 to 4	firm-fleshed fish steaks, such as salmon, grouper or halibut, at least 1 inch (2.5 cm) thick, about 2 lbs (1 kg)	2 to 4

1. Finely grate peel from lemon and orange. Squeeze juice from lemon. In a small bowl, stir peels with lemon juice, garlic, parsley, salt and olive oil. Place fish in a resealable plastic bag or dish with high sides just large enough to hold fish snugly, such as an 8-inch (2-L) baking dish. Coat both sides of steaks with parsley mixture. Seal bag or cover dish. Refrigerate from 2 to 4 hours. Turn bag or fish in dish at least once while marinating.

2. When ready to serve, preheat barbecue and oil grill. Lift fish from marinade and drain slightly. Place on hot grill. Baste occasionally with marinade from 5 to 6 minutes. Then turn fish. Immediately baste once, then discard remaining marinade. Continue grilling until fish is golden-tinged and a knife point inserted into centre of fish feels warm, from 5 to 6 more minutes. Serve with couscous or other small pasta and grilled vegetables such as tomatoes, zucchini and peppers.

MAKES: 4 to 6 servings

PREPARATION TIME: 10 minutes / MARINATING TIME: 2 hours

BARBECUING TIME: 10 minutes

Nutrients per serving: 23.4 g protein, 19.6 g total fat (3.5 g saturated, 66 mg cholesterol), 2.6 g carbohydrates, 0.7 mg iron, 32 mg calcium, 209 mg sodium, 0.8 g fibre, 285 calories

Excellent source of vitamins B_6 and B_{12}.
Good source of folic acid.

Hoisin Salmon au Poivre

This is an easy entertaining entrée to barbecue or roast. A fast stir-and-brush hoisin mixture dresses up salmon for the poshest of parties. Hoisin is a mixture of soybeans, garlic, chilies and other spices and has a slightly sweet taste.

½ cup	hoisin sauce	125 mL
2 tbsp	sherry, port or Marsala	30 mL
1½ tsp	coarsely ground black pepper	7 mL
6 to 8	skinless salmon fillets, centre-cut, about 1½ inches (3.5 cm) thick, or steaks, about 1 inch (2.5 cm) thick	6 to 8

1. Stir hoisin with sherry and pepper in a small bowl. To cook salmon, either preheat oven to 450°F (230°C) or oil barbecue grill, then preheat barbecue. Cook using one of the methods below. Then serve salmon right away with boiled new potatoes or rice pilaf and steamed asparagus or broccoli.

To roast: Line a baking sheet with shallow sides, such as a jelly roll pan, with foil. Then oil or coat foil with cooking spray since salmon tends to stick. Brush sauce all over salmon, including sides. Roast, uncovered and without turning, in centre of preheated oven for 10 minutes per inch (2.5 cm) of thickness. If fish is 1½ inches (3.5 cm) thick, it will need 15 minutes of roasting.

To barbecue: Brush sauce all over salmon, including sides. If preheated grill looks very dry, brush again with vegetable oil. Place salmon on very hot preheated grill. If using fillets, grill the pink side first by placing skin-side up on barbecue. Grill 7 minutes per side for thick fillets and 5 minutes per side for steaks. When turning fish, use a large wide spatula to avoid breaking fillet or steak.

MAKES: 6 to 8 servings
PREPARATION TIME: 5 minutes
ROASTING OR BARBECUING TIME: 15 minutes

Nutrients per serving: 29.9 g protein, 16.9 g total fat (3.4 g saturated, 84 mg cholesterol), 7.5 g carbohydrates, 0.7 mg iron, 78 mg calcium, 341 mg sodium, 0.5 g fibre, 313 calories

Excellent source of vitamins B6 and B12.
Good source of folic acid.

Health Wonders

Fish and Depression

Food may be good medicine for manic depression. In a recent study, patients who supplemented their daily drug therapy with 9 grams of omega-3 fatty acids from fish oil had fewer manic episodes and less depression than those who continued their regular drug treatment. These fatty acids may inhibit overactive pathways in the central nervous system and also have antidepressant effects.

Cooking with Fatty Fish

The omega-3s are one family of fatty acids, which are the building blocks of fats. The name omega-3 relates to the particular type of chemical linkage that holds these fatty acids together in the fat molecule.

Although omega-3 fatty acids are also found in plants and seed oils, the omega-3 fatty acids found in cold-water fish and fish oils are those that are most closely related to heart health. Fish is the recommended source because it directly provides the type of omega-3s that are believed to benefit the heart.

Understanding more about the science of cooking often means choosing to prepare foods in ways that preserve their nutritional content. For example, because omega-3 fatty acids are polyunsaturated, they deteriorate quickly when exposed to oxygen, light and heat. Therefore, you'll want to buy fish that is as fresh as possible and then use it right away.

Cold-water fish are a treat to cook because their fat adds rich appealing flavours and holds moisture in the muscle tissue. And they're well suited to high-temperature roasting, broiling, pan-frying and barbecuing – cooking methods that can leave lean fish quite dry.

Moroccan Fish Steaks

At Ottawa's Lapointe's Fresh Fish Café, fish steaks are marinated in an exotic combination of spices, then quickly grilled to golden-crusted perfection. Plunging your fork through the crust into the moist interior yields a truly wonderful taste and texture contrast.

4	salmon or halibut steaks, at least 1 inch (2.5 cm) thick	4
1 tbsp	each of coriander, cumin, caraway and fennel or anise seeds	15 mL
¼ cup	olive oil	50 mL
2 tsp	curry powder	10 mL
2 tsp	liquid honey	10 mL

1. Place steaks in a single layer in an 8-inch (2-L) square baking dish or in a resealable plastic bag. Mix seeds and coarsely grind (see Tip, below). Stir oil with ground seeds, curry powder and honey. Spread over both sides of steaks, letting some drizzle down sides. Cover or seal bag. Marinate in the refrigerator for at least 4 hours, preferably overnight. For a crusty exterior, don't skimp on marinating time. Turn steaks once while marinating.

2. When ready to grill, preheat barbecue and oil grill. Remove steaks from marinade. Carefully place on hot grill so spice coating remains intact. Barbecue, turning once, until crust is golden and fish is cooked as you like, from 5 to 6 minutes per side. Serve right away with couscous or rice.

MAKES: 4 servings
PREPARATION TIME: 10 minutes / MARINATING TIME: 4 hours
BARBECUING TIME: 10 minutes

TIP: To grind seeds, use a blender, electric coffee grinder or mortar and pestle. For best results with a blender or coffee grinder, whirl all the seeds at once.

Nutrients per serving: 26.8 g protein, 25.5 g total fat (4.3 g saturated, 74 mg cholesterol), 4.8 g carbohydrates, 2 mg iron, 61 mg calcium, 76 mg sodium, 0.4 g fibre, 357 calories

Excellent source of vitamins B6 and B12.
Good source of folic acid.

Roasted Sesame-Teriyaki Tuna Steaks

Serve these full-flavoured fish steaks, which take less than 15 minutes, with rice or a noodle salad toss for a sumptuous change from meat and potatoes.

1 tbsp	teriyaki sauce, preferably light	15 mL
1 tsp	dark sesame oil	5 mL
1 tsp	liquid honey	5 mL
2	tuna, salmon or swordfish steaks, at least ¾ inch (2 cm) thick	2

1. Preheat oven to 450°F (230°C). In a small bowl, stir teriyaki with oil and honey until blended. Place fish in a lightly oiled baking dish just large enough to hold it.

2. Bake in centre of preheated oven, basting fish with pan juices partway through cooking, until a knife point inserted in centre of fish for 10 seconds feels warm, from 8 to 10 minutes for ¾-inch (2-cm) steak or 10 minutes for a 1-inch (2.5-cm) steak. Do not turn. (If you like your tuna rare, you may want to cut cooking time to 5 or 6 minutes.)

Broiling or barbecuing: Stir teriyaki sauce with oil and honey as instructed above. Lightly brush teriyaki mixture over both sides of fish. Place fish on a lightly oiled broiler pan or greased barbecue grill. Broil about 4 inches (10 cm) from preheated element or on barbecue grill turned to high with lid closed. During cooking, brush often with teriyaki mixture until fish is cooked through, from 2 to 3 minutes per side for rare tuna and from 4 to 5 minutes per side for salmon or swordfish.

MAKES: 2 servings

PREPARATION TIME: 5 minutes / BAKING TIME: 8 minutes

Nutrients per serving: 40.2 g protein, 10.6 g total fat (2.5 g saturated, 65 mg cholesterol), 4.3 g carbohydrates, 1.9 mg iron, 16 mg calcium, 412 mg sodium, 0 g fibre, 282 calories

Excellent source of vitamins A, B6 and B12.

Tuna Niçoise Steaks

Tuna steaks are expensive but our robust tomato-and-olive relish more than does them justice.

4	tuna steaks or other firm-fleshed fish steaks, about ½ lb (250 g) each	4
¼ cup	olive or vegetable oil	50 mL
2 tbsp	freshly squeezed lemon juice	30 mL
1 tsp	Dijon mustard	5 mL
2 tsp	anchovy paste	10 mL
1 tsp	dried basil	5 mL
2	ripe tomatoes	2
¼ cup	pitted black kalamata olives	50 mL
½ tsp	granulated sugar	2 mL

1. Oil grill and preheat barbecue to medium-high heat. Remove fish from the refrigerator. Whisk oil with lemon juice, mustard, anchovy paste and basil. Set aside.

2. Prepare relish by cutting tomatoes in half and squeezing out seeds and juice. Finely chop and place in a bowl. Finely chop olives and add. Stir in sugar and 2 tablespoons (30 mL) anchovy mixture.

3. Generously brush steaks with remaining oil mixture. Place on grill and barbecue with lid down for 5 minutes per side, turning carefully and brushing often with oil mixture.

4. Remove steaks to a platter. Pour any remaining oil mixture over top. Spoon fresh tomato-olive mixture over each steak. Great with herbed rice or couscous with green onions.

Indoor oven broiling: Prepare steaks as you would for barbecuing. Preheat broiler. Place oven rack about 4 inches (10 cm) from broiler. Brush fish with anchovy mixture and place on a broiling pan. Broil from 5 to 7 minutes per side, brushing often with mixture, until tip of a knife inserted in centre of fish feels warm.

MAKES: 4 servings

PREPARATION TIME: 15 minutes / GRILLING TIME: 10 minutes

Nutrients per serving: 54.1 g protein, 26.1 g total fat (4 g saturated, 88 mg cholesterol), 4.5 g carbohydrates, 3 mg iron, 39 mg calcium, 257 mg sodium, 1 g fibre, 477 calories

Excellent source of vitamins A, B6 and B12.
Good source of iron.

Halibut with Anchovies

This classic French fish preparation works beautifully with any firm-fleshed fish such as swordfish. We used halibut here and omega-3-loaded anchovies.

1 tbsp	each of butter and olive oil	15 mL
1½ lbs	halibut steaks, about 1 inch (2.5 cm) thick	750 g
¼ cup	all-purpose flour	50 mL
1 cup	dry white wine	250 mL
3	anchovy fillets, finely chopped or 1 tbsp (15 mL) anchovy paste	3
	freshly ground white pepper	
½	lemon	½
¼ cup	finely chopped fresh dill	50 mL

1. Heat butter and oil in a large wide frying pan over medium-high heat. Meanwhile, if necessary, cut halibut into 3 or 4 servings. Lightly coat with flour. Add fish to pan and cook over medium-high heat for about 2 minutes per side.

2. Immediately pour wine over fish. Add anchovies to wine mixture along with pepper. Mash anchovies into sauce, then whisk until evenly blended.

3. Adjust heat so wine boils gently. Cook halibut steaks, uncovered, from 2 to 3 more minutes per side or until fish is flaky. Remove fish to dinner plates. Increase heat to high and boil wine mixture, uncovered, until slightly thickened, about 2 minutes. Pour over fish. Squeeze lemon juice over top, then sprinkle with fresh dill. Serve with rice tossed with thinly sliced green onions and broccoli sprinkled with lemon pepper.

MAKES: 3 or 4 servings

PREPARATION TIME: 2 minutes / COOKING TIME: 10 minutes

Nutrients per serving: 30.6 g protein, 9.8 g total fat (2.8 g saturated, 55 mg cholesterol), 5 g carbohydrates, 1.8 mg iron, 81 mg calcium, 218 mg sodium, 0.2 g fibre, 264 calories

Excellent source of vitamins B6 and B12.

omega-3 fatty acids

vitamin B

iron

Seeds and nuts

Nuts and seeds are big players in slashing your risk of heart disease. Flaxseed offers a triple nutritional whammy and tastes good, too! It's a great source of plant-derived omega-3 fatty acids, known to help protect against heart disease, it's a great natural laxative and is now believed to have anti-cancer effects as well.

Nuts, although high in fat and calories, can be nutritious if enjoyed smartly. A long-term study showed that those eating nuts once a day reduced their risk of heart disease by almost 35 percent. That's because most of the fat in nuts is unsaturated, which helps control blood cholesterol.

Baked Homemade Granola

Most store-bought granola is high in fat and calories. Make your own granola and keep the fat content down, but the goodness of nuts and seeds high. Use it for everything from a healthy snack to a topping for yogurt or a baked apple.

4 cups	rolled oats	1 L
2 cups	mixed nuts and seeds such as pumpkin seeds, sunflower seeds, sesame seeds, slivered almonds and coarsely chopped walnuts	500 g
1 tsp	cinnamon	5 mL
½ tsp	nutmeg	2 mL
½	cup warm water	125 mL
½ cup	maple syrup	125 mL
½ tsp	vanilla	2 mL
1 cup	mix of raisins, chopped dried apricots and dates	250 g

1. Preheat oven to 300°F (150°C). Lightly oil two jelly roll pans or large cookie sheets. In a large bowl, stir oats with nuts, seeds and spices. Stir warm water with maple syrup and vanilla. While stirring, gradually pour into oat mixture and continue to mix until ingredients are evenly coated. Spread out on the two oiled pans and bake, stirring every 10 minutes to prevent burning, until granola is crumbly and golden in colour, about 30 minutes. Remove from the oven and immediately stir in raisin mixture. When cool, store in an airtight container for up to 5 days at room temperature or up to 1 month in the refrigerator.

MAKES: about 6 cups (1.5 mL)
PREPARATION TIME: 10 minutes / COOKING TIME: 30 minutes

BAKED APPLES: Preheat oven to 350°F (180°C). Remove cores from 4 unpeeled apples. Firmly pack each apple with about 2 tablespoons (30 mL) granola. Arrange in a baking dish. Sprinkle generously with cinnamon. Bake, uncovered, in preheated oven until tender, about 30 minutes. Serve with maple syrup and light sour cream or yogurt.

Nutrients per ¼ cup (50 mL): 4.6 g protein, 6.3 g total fat (0.9 g saturated, 0 mg cholesterol), 17.4 g carbohydrates, 1.6 mg iron, 26 mg calcium, 4 mg sodium, 2.7 g fibre, 137 calories

Good source of magnesium.
Moderate amount of dietary fibre.

Toasted Pecan Rice

Pecans, a source of zinc, which helps boost the immune system, join three of our favourite herbs in this side dish. For a vegetarian entrée, use vegetable broth in place of chicken broth.

4	thin or 2 thick leeks or 1 large onion	4
4	carrots	4
¼ to ½ cup	toasted pecan halves	50 to 125 mL
1 tbsp	butter	15 mL
3	minced garlic cloves	3
3 cups	chicken broth or bouillon	750 mL
½ tsp	salt	2 mL
1½ cups	long-grain rice, preferably converted	375 mL
1	stem fresh thyme or 1 tsp (5 mL) dried leaf thyme	1
4	large basil leaves or ½ tsp (2 mL) dried basil	4
¾ cup	snipped chives or 4 green onions, thinly sliced	175 mL

1. Peel and slice away tough dark leaves from leeks and discard. Slice in half lengthwise. Fan layers under cold running water to wash away sand. Then thinly slice. Chop or grate carrots. Coarsely chop pecans but leave a few whole. If using peanuts, leave whole.

2. Heat butter in a large saucepan over medium heat. Add leeks, carrots and garlic. Stir often until fragrant, about 5 minutes. Add broth and salt. Bring to a boil. Stir in rice. Submerge stem of fresh thyme in liquid or sprinkle in dried thyme. If not using fresh basil, add dried basil. Cover, reduce heat to low and simmer until rice is done as you like, from 20 to 25 minutes.

3. Stack fresh basil leaves and slice into shreds. When rice is done, remove and discard thyme stem. Stir in basil, chives and nuts. Great with roast turkey or pork. Rice will keep well, covered in the refrigerator, for at least 2 days.

Make ahead: Place cooked hot rice in a casserole dish and cover. Wrap with a towel if serving within an hour. Warm rice, if needed, in a covered casserole dish in a 350°F (180°C) oven, stirring every 10 minutes, until hot. Or warm in microwave on medium power, covered and stirring every 5 minutes.

MAKES: 7 cups (1.75 L), about 6 servings

PREPARATION TIME: 20 minutes / COOKING TIME: 25 minutes

Nutrients per cup (250 mL): 7.7 g protein, 6.6 g total fat (1.8 g saturated, 5 mg cholesterol), 49.3 g carbohydrates, 1.9 mg iron, 83 mg calcium, 644 mg sodium, 4.2 g fibre, 286 calories

Excellent source of vitamin A.
Good source of vitamin B6 and folic acid.
High amount of dietary fibre.

Maple-Banana Bread with Flax

Potassium-rich bananas flavour but don't overpower this nutty bread. It's also one of the most delicious ways we know to enjoy the triple nutritional whammy of flaxseeds. The grain, rich in omega-3 fatty acids, is a natural laxative, it helps protect against heart disease by lowering cholesterol and it is now believed to have anti-cancer effects as well.

1 cup	all-purpose flour	250 mL
¾ cup	whole wheat flour	175 mL
2½ tsp	baking powder	12 mL
½ tsp	baking soda	2 mL
½ tsp	cinnamon	2 mL
½ tsp	salt	2 mL
¼ tsp	ground ginger	1 mL
¼ cup	flaxseed, ground or toasted and crushed	50 mL
¼ cup	toasted chopped walnuts or pecans	50 mL
2	eggs	2
1 cup	very ripe bananas, mashed (about 2)	250 mL
½ cup	maple syrup	125 mL
3 tbsp	vegetable oil or melted butter	45 mL
½ tsp	vanilla	2 mL

1. Preheat oven to 350°F (180°C). Lightly butter a 9x5-inch (1.5-L) loaf pan or coat with cooking spray. In a large bowl, using a fork, stir flours with baking powder, baking soda, cinnamon, salt and ginger until blended. Stir in ground flaxseed or if using whole flaxseeds, toast in a dry skillet over medium-high, shaking often, from 3 to 4 minutes. Crush, then stir into flour mixture with nuts. Make a well in centre.

2. In a mixing bowl, lightly beat eggs, then stir in mashed banana, syrup, oil and vanilla until blended. Pour into well in flour mixture. Stir just until evenly mixed. Immediately pour batter into prepared pan and smooth the top. Bake in centre of 350°F (180°C) oven until a cake tester inserted in the centre right to the bottom comes out clean, about 50 minutes. Let stand 5 minutes in pan on a rack. Then turn out on rack to cool. Loaf will keep well at room temperature for up to 3 days or can be frozen.

MAKES: 18 slices

PREPARATION TIME: 15 minutes / BAKING TIME: 50 minutes

Nutrients per slice: 2.9 g protein, 4.9 g total fat (0.6 g saturated, 24 mg cholesterol), 18.9 g carbohydrates, 1 mg iron, 36 mg calcium, 142 mg sodium, 1.5 g fibre, 127 calories

Good source of plant-derived omega-3 fatty acids.

Health Wonders

Flax Facts

Fibre

Because flaxseed contains soluble fibre, it makes you feel full sooner, so you may end up eating less of other, not-so-nutritious foods. Fibre also keeps reluctant bowels moving and lowers blood cholesterol, thereby reducing risk of heart disease.

Heart Health

Flaxseed is rich in alpha-linolenic acid (ALA), one of the now-famous omega-3 polyunsaturated fatty acids. ALA reduces the risk of heart disease by reducing platelet stickiness, which in turn reduces blood clotting. Two studies on flaxseed consumption from University of Toronto researchers showed that when 50 grams a day were given to healthy people with normal cholesterol levels, serum cholesterol went down by 6 percent and LDL cholesterol (low-density lipoprotein, the "bad" cholesterol) went down by 9 percent.

Possible Anti-cancer Effects

If regularity and a healthier heart aren't enough to win you over, flaxseed also contains lignans, which appear to have anti-cancer effects. The lignan content of flaxseed is up to 100 to 800 times greater than that of other plant foods such as legumes, veggies and cereal grains. Recent research on breast cancer patients has shown dramatic results. Researchers at Toronto's Princess Margaret Hospital found a "slowing down in tumour growth" when they studied breast cancer patients fed flaxseed muffins. Fifty women who had recently been diagnosed with cancer and who were awaiting removal of their tumours, were divided into two groups — one group received a daily muffin containing 2 tablespoons (30 mL) of ground flaxseed, the others ate muffins without flaxseeds. When the tumours were removed, approximately 35 days after diagnosis, the women who had received the flaxseed muffins had slower-growing tumours than the others. Recommended daily intake for healthy women is 1 to 2 tablespoons (15 to 30 mL) of ground flaxseed.

Nuts and Heart Disease

Nuts get a bad rap for their high-fat content but they may cut women's risk of heart disease. In a study published in the *British Medical Journal*, researchers followed 86,000 women for 14 years and found that women who ate at least one ounce (30 grams) of nuts a day had a 35 percent lower risk of developing heart disease. Raw nuts contain mainly unsaturated fat, which has beneficial effects on blood lipids by lowering total and LDL cholesterol, say researchers.

Fabulous Flax Muffins

These little muffins give you so much goodness — both in taste and health. The most recent research showed women eating flax-filled muffins slowed the growth of their breast tumours. Each muffin here contains two tablespoons (30 mL) ground flaxseed — a commendable amount of this valuable seed.

1½ cups	ground flaxseeds	375 mL
½ cup	whole wheat flour	125 mL
½ cup	all-purpose flour	125 mL
½ cup	brown sugar	125 mL
4 tsp	baking powder	20 mL
1 tsp	cinnamon	5 mL
½ tsp	each nutmeg and salt	2 mL
1½ cups	milk, preferably skim	375 mL
2 tbsp	olive oil	30 mL
1	egg	1
	finely grated peel of 1 orange	
½ tsp	vanilla	2 mL
1½ cups	golden raisins	375 mL

1. Preheat oven to 350°F (180°C). Grease 12 muffin cups or coat with cooking spray. In a large bowl, using a fork, stir flaxseeds with whole wheat flour, all-purpose flour, brown sugar, baking powder, cinnamon, nutmeg and salt until evenly blended. In a medium-size bowl, using a fork, whisk milk with olive oil, egg, orange peel and vanilla just until blended. Pour milk mixture into flour mixture and stir just until combined. Stir in raisins.

2. Spoon mixture into each muffin cup filling about ¾ full. Bake on centre rack of preheated oven until a toothpick inserted in centre comes out clean and top is firm to the touch, about 25 minutes. Let stand for 5 minutes before removing from cups. Muffins are delicious warm spread with strawberry jam.

MAKES: 12 small muffins

PREPARATION TIME: 15 minutes / BAKING TIME: 25 minutes

TIP: Healthy additions: In place of the raisins, add about ½ (125 mL) cup dried cranberries and ¾ cup coarsely chopped walnuts.

Nutrients per muffin: 7.1 g protein, 9.8 g total fat (1.2 g saturated fat, 18 mg cholesterol) 41.9 g carbohydrates, 3.4 mg iron, 158 mg calcium, 222 mg sodium, 5.8 g fibre, 270 calories

Excellent source of folic acid and magnesium.
Good source of iron.
High amount of dietary fibre.

Crunchy Pecan Lime Chicken

Add a healthy nut coating to chicken instead of bread crumbs. The pecans are crunchy, a source of zinc, and miles ahead of soggy bread.

4	skinless, boneless chicken breasts	4
1	egg, beaten	1
	juice and grated peel from ½ lime	
pinch	cayenne pepper	pinch
¼ cup	finely chopped pecans	50 mL
1 tbsp	butter	15 mL

1. Whisk egg in a shallow bowl. Stir in grated peel and juice from ½ lime and cayenne pepper.

2. Place nuts in a shallow bowl. Dip chicken, one breast at a time, into beaten egg mixture, then press finely chopped pecans into chicken.

3. Melt butter in a large frying pan over medium heat. Add the chicken and sauté, from 6 to 8 minutes per side.

MAKES: 2 to 4 servings

PREPARATION TIME: 10 minutes / COOKING TIME: 12 minutes

Nutrients per serving: 34 g protein, 10.8 g total fat (3.1 g saturated, 132 mg cholesterol), 1.8 g carbohydrates, 0.8 mg iron, 14 mg calcium, 114 mg sodium, 0.5 g fibre, 246 calories

Excellent source of vitamin B_6.
Good source of vitamin B_{12}.

Almond Chicken Stir-Fry

Many of us avoid nuts, all too aware of their high-calorie count. But almonds, rich in calcium and vitamin E, a powerful antioxidant which reduces the risk of heart disease, deserve a place on your table. For a healthy one-dish dinner with a minimum of fuss, serve this easy stir-fry. You also get calcium from both the green beans and the bok choy.

4	skinless, boneless chicken breasts	4
1	onion, thinly sliced	1
2	minced garlic cloves	2
¼ to ⅓ cup	soy or teriyaki sauce	50 to 75 mL
1	sweet red pepper	1
4 cups	fresh or frozen green beans	1 L
1	small bok choy or 2 cups (500 mL) shredded cabbage	1
1 tbsp	vegetable oil	15 mL
1 tbsp	grated fresh ginger or bottled ginger or ½ tsp (2 mL) ground ginger	15 mL
¾ tsp	hot red chili flakes	3 mL
1 to 2 tbsp	water	15 to 30 mL
½ to 1 cup	whole blanched almonds, toasted	125 to 250 mL

1. Have all ingredients prepared before starting to stir-fry. Slice chicken into ½-inch (1-cm) strips. Place chicken, onion and garlic in a large bowl. Add 2 tablespoons (30 mL) soy sauce and stir until chicken is evenly coated. Seed pepper and slice into bite-size strips. Trim fresh beans or rinse frozen beans with cold water to remove ice crystals. Then drain. Slice bok choy into bite-size pieces.

2. When ready to stir-fry, heat oil in a wide saucepan over medium heat. When hot, add chicken mixture. Sauté, stirring often, about 2 minutes. Add ginger and hot red chili flakes. Stir often for 5 minutes. Then add peppers, beans and water. Stir-fry just until beans are bright green, from 4 to 5 minutes. Add bok choy and remaining soy. Toss until bok choy is hot, about 2 minutes. Sprinkle almonds over top and serve.

MAKES: 4 servings

PREPARATION TIME: 20 minutes / COOKING TIME: 13 minutes

Nutrients per serving: 35.5 g protein, 15.4 g total fat (1.7 g saturated, 68 mg cholesterol), 19.7 g carbohydrates, 3.9 mg iron, 159 mg calcium, 1,127 mg sodium, 5.5 g fibre, 346 calories

Excellent source of vitamins A, C and B6, folic acid and iron.
Good source of vitamin B12.
High amount of dietary fibre.

Orange-Rhubarb Walnut Loaf

Prairie cook Pat Thompson of Assiniboia, Saskatchewan, freezes her garden rhubarb for this
healthy loaf loaded with rhubarb fibre, vitamin C from oranges and omega-3 from walnuts.

2½ cups	sliced frozen or 2 cups (500 mL) fresh rhubarb	625 mL
¼ cup	granulated sugar	50 mL
2 to 3	oranges	2 to 3
2 tbsp	granulated sugar	30 mL
1	egg	1
1 tsp	vanilla	5 mL
3 cups	all-purpose flour	750 mL
¾ cup	granulated sugar	175 mL
3 tsp	baking powder	3 mL
1 tsp	baking soda	5 mL
½ tsp	salt	2 mL
⅓ cup	butter, melted and cooled	75 mL
¾ cup	walnuts or pecans, coarsely chopped	175 mL

1. Measure out rhubarb. Defrost if frozen and pat dry. Finely chop. Preheat oven to 350°F (180°C). Lightly grease a 9x5-inch (1.5-L) loaf pan. Stir rhubarb with ¼ cup (50 mL) sugar. Finely grate 2 tablespoons (30 mL) peel from 2 oranges and squeeze out 1 cup (250 mL) juice. Measure 2 tablespoons (30 mL) juice into a small dish. Stir in 2 tablespoons (30 mL) sugar and set aside to glaze loaf.

2. In a medium-size bowl, beat egg. Stir in remaining juice, grated peel and vanilla. Measure flour, ¾ cup (175 m L) sugar, baking powder, soda and salt into a large bowl. Stir with a fork until blended and make a well in centre. Pour in egg mixture and butter. Stir just until evenly combined. Batter is thick. Stir in rhubarb mixture and nuts just until distributed.

3. Turn into prepared pan. Batter will almost fill pan. Smooth top. Bake in centre of preheated oven until a skewer inserted into centre comes out clean, about 75 minutes. Remove to a rack. Stir orange juice and sugar mixture. Spoon over top of hot loaf. Cool in pan 10 minutes. Turn out of pan and finish cooling on rack. Loaf will keep well, covered, at room temperature for 2 days. Or wrap airtight and freeze.

MAKES: 12 slices

PREPARATION TIME: 25 minutes / BAKING TIME: 75 minutes

Nutrients per slice: 4.7 g protein, 10.8 g total fat (3.8 g saturated, 32 mg cholesterol), 48.1 g carbohydrates, 1.7 mg iron, 96 mg calcium, 317 mg sodium, 2.1 g fibre, 304 calories

Good source of folic acid.
Moderate amount of dietary fibre.

calcium

phytoestrogens

fibre

Soy

protein

Soy foods are staples in Asian countries where
breast and prostate cancer rates are much
lower than in Canada. Soybeans and soy
protein products, including tofu, miso, tempeh
and soy drinks, contain phytoestrogens that
slow the growth of some cancers, help relieve
menopausal symptoms, lower cholesterol and
offer some protection against osteoporosis.

isoflavones

Caesar Salad Dressing with Tofu

Guilt-free Caesar dressing is made creamy and healthy with silken tofu instead of oil. Toss with romaine and croutons or use as a rich healthy dip for pepper and cucumber sticks.

½	(10-oz/290-g) pkg silken tofu	½
2 tbsp	freshly squeezed lemon juice	30 mL
2 tbsp	water	30 mL
1 tbsp	olive oil	15 mL
1 tsp	anchovy paste or 1 anchovy fillet	5 mL
¼ tsp	each of salt and pepper	2 mL
2 tbsp	freshly grated Parmesan	30 mL

1. Place all ingredients, except Parmesan, in a blender jar or food processor. Whirl until smooth, stopping and scraping down sides once. Add Parmesan and whirl until mixed. Toss with romaine lettuce, croutons and more Parmesan or use as a great dip. Refrigerated, dressing will keep for 3 days.

MAKES: 1 cup (250 mL)

PREPARATION TIME: 5 minutes

Nutrients per tablespoon (15 mL): 0.8 g protein, 1.4 g total fat (0.4 g saturated, 1 mg cholesterol), 0.4 g carbohydrates, 0.1 mg iron, 14 mg calcium, 60 mg sodium, 0.1 g fibre, 17 calories

Spicy Tofu Burritos

These burritos take only 5 minutes to cook and are loaded with all the healthy goodness that eating soy foods provide such as lowering blood cholesterol.

12-oz	pkg firm or soft tofu, drained	350-g
2 tbsp	olive oil	30 mL
1	small onion, chopped, about ½ cup (125 mL)	1
1	sweet red pepper, seeded and finely chopped	1
1	small jalapeño, seeded and minced	1
2	minced garlic cloves	2
1 tsp	chili powder	5 mL
1 tsp	ground cumin	5 mL
½ tsp	dried leaf oregano	2 mL
pinch	salt and freshly ground black pepper	pinch
¼ cup	finely chopped coriander	50 mL
2 tbsp	salsa	30 mL
4	flour tortillas (7 to 8 inches/17 to 20 cm)	4
	shredded cheddar cheese and lettuce, chopped tomatoes and low-fat sour cream for toppings	

1. Slice firm tofu in strips, about ½ inch (1 cm) thick and 2 inches (5 cm) long, and set aside. Heat oil in a large non-stick frying pan over medium-high heat. Add onion and stir until it softens slightly, about 2 minutes. Add tofu strips or coarsely crumble in soft tofu. Then add red pepper, jalapeño and garlic. Sprinkle with chili powder, cumin, oregano, salt and pepper. Stir-fry until heated through, from 3 to 4 minutes. Stir in coriander.

2. Spoon tofu filling evenly down the centre of each warmed tortilla (see Tip, below). Top with salsa and whatever other toppings you like. Wrap tortilla around filling and serve.

MAKES: 4 burritos

PREPARATION TIME: 20 minutes / COOKING TIME: 5 minutes

TIP: To warm tortillas, wrap in foil and place in preheated 350°F (180°C) oven until warm. Or stack tortillas on a paper towel in the microwave and warm on high for 30 seconds.

Nutrients per burrito: 11.5 g protein, 13.9 g total fat (1.9 g saturated, 0 mg cholesterol), 31.6 g carbohydrates, 3.4 mg iron, 176 mg calcium, 240 mg sodium, 2.8 g fibre, 288 calories

Excellent source of vitamin C.
Good source of vitamin A, folic acid, calcium and iron.
Moderate amount of dietary fibre.

Tempeh Fajitas

Tempeh, made from pressed whole soybeans, has about 20 percent more protein than tofu. Its assertive soy flavour takes on the taste of the other ingredients, so expect a kick from the chili and lime in this recipe. Its chewy meat-like texture is especially popular with vegetarians.

8-oz	pkg frozen tempeh	250-g
1	lime or ½ lemon	1
4 tsp	soy sauce	20 mL
1 tbsp	water	15 mL
2 tbsp	vegetable oil	30 mL
1	onion, thinly sliced	1
2	minced garlic cloves	2
1	sweet pepper, thinly sliced	1
½ tsp	chili powder	2 mL
¼ cup	water	50 mL
4	flour tortillas, about 6 inches (12 cm) wide	4

1. Unwrap frozen tempeh and cut in half. Slice into bite-size strips, about ½ inch (1 cm) wide. Finely grate peel from lime and squeeze out 2 tablespoons (30 mL) juice. Stir with soy sauce and 1 tablespoon (15 mL) water in a medium-size dish. Stir in tempeh. Cover and marinate, turning strips occasionally, for 1 hour at room temperature or overnight in the refrigerator.

2. Then heat 1 tablespoon (15 mL) oil in a large frying pan over medium heat. Add tempeh and sauté for 2 minutes per side. Remove when golden. Add 1 tablespoon (15 mL) oil to pan. When hot, add onion, garlic, pepper and chili powder. Sauté, stirring often, until onion is soft, about 5 minutes. Add tempeh and ¼ cup (50 mL) water. Stir until hot, about 2 minutes. Roll in tortillas. Top with sour cream and salsa.

MAKES: 4 fajitas

PREPARATION TIME: 10 minutes / MARINATING TIME: 1 hour
COOKING TIME: 12 minutes

Nutrients per serving: 14.5 g protein, 13.5 g total fat (1.5 g saturated, 0 mg cholesterol), 33.1 g carbohydrates, 2.7 mg iron, 78 mg calcium, 417 mg sodium, 2 g fibre, 301 calories

Excellent source of vitamin B12.
Good source of vitamins C and B6 and folic acid.
Moderate amount of dietary fibre.

Health Wonders

Soy Good

Whether you call them tofu or bean curd, those custard-like white blocks sold in most supermarkets can help you serve a healthy meal in record time. The Japanese count on tofu as a dietary mainstay. Now, this protein-rich soybean product is winning fans in North America. While it's short on taste and aroma, tofu takes little prep time, absorbs flavours beautifully and fits easily into mainstream meals (no exotic fixings required.)

Tofu is made from soy milk by a process similar to cheese production. You can find tofu in the refrigerated produce section of the supermarket. Firm tofu works best for stir-fries and stews while silken tofu is good for dressings, spreads and desserts. As well as providing protein, tofu can be an excellent source of iron and calcium if the soy is fortified. A $3\frac{1}{2}$-oz (100-g) serving has 1 g carbohydrates, 4 g fat, 7 g protein and 69 calories.

Silken Tofu
Silken tofu is sold in supermarkets in boxes similar to juice-drink boxes. Its silky texture and mild soy flavour work well in dressings, sauces and shakes.

Tempeh
Tempeh, made from pressed whole soybeans, has a thin white coating covered with black flecks. Broiled or sautéed, it has an assertive soy flavour and will take on the taste of other ingredients.

Soy Beverages
Soy milk has a smooth creamy texture and mild sweetness and comes in a variety of flavours including chocolate and vanilla. It is made by puréeing soybeans in water and cooking the strained liquid under special conditions to remove the bean flavour. Soy milk is a good source of protein, B vitamins and iron; it's low in saturated fat and cholesterol-free; and many brands are now fortified with calcium. In some recipes, soy beverages can be substituted for milk.

Hot-and-Sour Soup

This shimmering soup full of tofu and mushrooms takes mere minutes to make. Our version skips the cornstarch that makes some commercial varieties of this Asian favourite so thick and gloppy.

10-oz	can chicken broth	284-mL
3 cups	water	750 mL
2 tbsp	minced fresh ginger	30 mL
	or 1½ tsp (7 mL) grated fresh ginger	
⅓-oz	pkg dried sliced mushrooms, such as porcini	10-g
1 tbsp	soy sauce	15 mL
2 tbsp	rice vinegar	30 mL
1 tsp	granulated sugar	5 mL
½ to 1 tsp	hot chili-garlic sauce or hot pepper sauce	2 to 5 mL
1 tsp	dark sesame oil	5 mL
½-inch	bundle of very thin rice-stick noodles, about ⅔ oz (20 g)	1-cm
6 oz	silken tofu, bay scallops or shrimp	180 g
3	green onions	3

1. Combine broth, water and ginger in a large saucepan. Then rinse mushrooms under cold running water and add. Stir in soy sauce, vinegar, sugar, ½ teaspoon (2 mL) chili-garlic sauce and sesame oil. Bring to a boil.

2. Break noodles so they measure about 4 inches (10 cm) long. Add to soup. Simmer over medium heat, uncovered, just until noodles are as tender as you like, about 8 minutes. Meanwhile, dice tofu or peel shrimp. Thinly slice onions diagonally. Stir tofu, scallops or shrimp into soup once noodles are almost tender. Continue simmering, covered, just until tofu is hot, scallops are opaque or shrimp are bright pink, about 3 minutes. Stir in onions. Taste and add more chili-garlic sauce for fire or vinegar for zip, if you like.

MAKES: 4 cups (1 L)

PREPARATION TIME: 10 minutes / COOKING TIME: 15 minutes

Nutrients per cup (250 mL): 7.2 g protein, 3.3 g total fat (1 g saturated, 1 mg cholesterol), 10.9 g carbohydrates, 1.1 mg iron, 29 mg calcium, 762 mg sodium, 1.5 g fibre, 98 calories

Tofu, Spinach and Pepper Stir-Fry

This highly flavoured entrée is a great way to introduce high-protein tofu into your diet.

12-oz	pkg extra-firm tofu	350-g
2 tbsp	freshly squeezed lemon juice	30 mL
1 tbsp	cornstarch	15 mL
1	onion	1
2	sweet red peppers	2
10-oz	pkg or 1 or 2 bunches regular or baby spinach	284-g
2 tbsp	vegetable oil	30 mL
2	minced garlic cloves	2
¼ to ½ tsp	hot red chili flakes	1 to 2 mL
½ tsp	salt	2 mL
¼ tsp	black pepper	1 mL
2 tsp	capers	10 mL

1. Cut drained tofu into ½-inch (1-cm) cubes. In a small mixing bowl, stir lemon juice with cornstarch. Then add tofu and toss until evenly coated. Let sit, uncovered and stirring occasionally, for 1 hour so lemon flavour permeates tofu.

2. Thinly slice onion. Seed and slice peppers into thin strips. If using regular spinach, remove and discard stems. Tear leaves into halves or quarters. Leave baby spinach whole, including tender stems. You should have about 7 cups (1.75 L). Have all vegetables prepared and ingredients measured before beginning to stir-fry.

3. Heat oil in a large frying pan or wok over medium-high heat. Add onion, garlic and chili flakes. Stir for 1 minute. Add peppers and sprinkle with salt and pepper. Continue stir-frying until peppers are hot, about 2 minutes. Add tofu and gently stir-fry until hot, about 1 minute. Add capers, then spinach in handfuls as needed, stirring until all spinach has wilted, about 1 more minute. Serve right away over hot rice.

MAKES: 4 servings
PREPARATION TIME: 20 minutes / MARINATING TIME: 1 hour
COOKING TIME: 5 minutes

Nutrients per serving: 11.7 g protein, 12.4 g total fat (1.3 g saturated, 0 mg cholesterol), 13.4 g carbohydrates, 4.1 mg iron, 223 mg calcium, 365 mg sodium, 2 g fibre, 195 calories

Excellent source of vitamins A and C and folic acid. **Good source of** vitamin B6 and calcium. **Moderate amount of** dietary fibre.

Orange-Teriyaki Broccoli Tofu Toss

Known as "meat of the fields" by the Japanese, tofu is a great high-protein alternative to meat. Pair it with broccoli and you have a meal that not only helps lower "bad" LDL cholesterol, but gives you some vitamin C and folic acid, too.

8-oz	pkg extra-firm tofu or chicken, sliced into strips	250-g
4 tbsp	teriyaki sauce	60 mL
1	medium-size onion	1
1 cup	chicken or vegetable broth	250 mL
2 tbsp	frozen orange juice concentrate	30 mL
1	minced garlic glove	1
½ tsp	salt	2 mL
2 tsp	cornstarch	10 mL
1 tbsp	vegetable oil	15 mL
4 cups	small broccoli florets, about 1 large bunch	1 L
1	small red pepper, diced	1
2 tsp	sesame oil	10 mL
4	green onions, thinly sliced	4
1 to 2 tsp	hot chili-garlic sauce (optional)	5 to 10 mL

1. Place tofu or chicken in a bowl. You should have about 2 cups (500 mL). Stir in 2 tablespoons (30 mL) teriyaki sauce until coated. Slice onion in half, then into thin semicircles. In another bowl, stir broth with orange juice concentrate, remaining teriyaki, garlic, salt and cornstarch until dissolved.

2. Heat vegetable oil in a large deep frying pan over medium-high heat. Remove tofu or chicken from the marinade. Place in pan, along with onion. Stir-fry just until tofu browns or chicken turns golden, about 5 minutes. Stir in broccoli and orange juice mixture, then stir for 2 minutes. Add pepper and continue to stir until sauce is thickened and broccoli is tender, from 2 to 4 more minutes. Stir in sesame oil and green onions. Stir in chili-garlic sauce to taste. Serve over hot Oriental noodles, spaghetti or rice.

MAKES: 5 cups (1.25 L) sauce to coat ½ lb (250 g) pasta
PREPARATION TIME: 10 minutes / COOKING TIME: 10 minutes

Nutrients per 2 cups (500 mL) sauce: 16.9 protein, 15.7 g total fat (1.9 g saturated, 0 mg cholesterol), 25.8 g carbohydrates, 3.5 mg iron, 212 mg calcium, 1,818 mg sodium, 4.1 g fibre, 292 calories

Excellent source of vitamins A and C and folic acid. **Good source of** vitamin B6 and calcium. **High amount of** dietary fibre.

Health Wonders

Soy and Menopause

Soy contains isoflavones, compounds that mimic the natural estrogens in our bodies. Studies show that they can diminish the intensity of hot flashes and may provide protection for our hearts. More importantly, the research also suggests that isoflavones inhibit the negative effect that estrogen has on the breasts and uterus. We're talking dietary soy here. Recent research from the Mayo Clinic found that soy supplements were not effective in reducing menopausal symptoms. Soy advocates are quick to point out that isoflavones in supplements cannot be assumed to have the same effects as dietary soy.

Experts recommend at least a daily serving of soy products, which may include 125 grams of tofu, one to two (8-oz/250-mL) glasses of soy milk, or 20 to 30 grams of soy protein mixed in with your favourite drink. Other lesser sources of isoflavones include whole grains (rye, wheat or flax) and legumes (beans and peas).

Ordering Chinese

For years, Asian diets have been winning praise for being heart-healthy. A new study proves the protective effects of a regimen rich in rice, vegetables, tofu and green tea. Cardiologists compared 116 men and women living in and outside of China and discovered that those eating a typical "American diet" that included more meat, dairy products and deep-fried foods had higher odds of developing cardiovascular problems. Westernized Chinese men and women were at increased risk of stroke and heart disease.

Soy and Cholesterol

Besides the fact that soy is a good source of protein and protects against heart disease and menopausal symptoms, new research suggests yet another reason to eat it. The soybean may also lower cholesterol, according to the *Archives of Internal Medicine*. In a study of 156 men and women with high levels of LDL – the bad cholesterol – those who ate 25 grams of soy protein a day for nine weeks experienced drops as high as 10 percent in LDL levels.

Speedy Couscous Supper

Couscous, a pale golden, granular grain, is a staple of North African cuisine. Since it only takes minutes to make, this handy recipe will let you pull dinner together quickly right out of the fridge.

2 cups	dry couscous or 12-oz (340-g) pkg	500 mL
2 cups	diced extra-firm tofu or cooked lean chicken, ham or beef	500 mL
2	grated peeled carrots or 1 small chopped zucchini or 1 thinly sliced celery stalk	2
2 cups	orange juice	500 mL
¼ cup	chopped fresh basil or 1 tsp (5 mL) dried basil (optional)	50 mL
2	finely chopped green onions or ¼ cup (50 mL) finely chopped red onion	2
½ tsp	salt	2 mL
½ tsp	freshly ground black pepper	2 mL

1. Place couscous, tofu and carrots in a large heatproof serving bowl. Heat orange juice in a saucepan over high heat or in a microwave until boiling. Stir into couscous. Cover tightly with a plate, a piece of foil or plastic wrap. Let stand for 5 minutes. Then sprinkle with basil, onions, salt and pepper. Stir gently until evenly mixed.

MAKES: 4 servings

PREPARATION TIME: 5 minutes / COOKING TIME: 3 minutes

Nutrients per serving: 22.2 g protein, 6.1 g total fat (0.9 g saturated, 0 mg cholesterol), 90.9 g carbohydrates, 3.2 mg iron, 181 mg calcium, 338 mg sodium, 6 g fibre, 503 calories

Excellent source of vitamins A and C and folic acid. **Good source of** vitamin B6 and calcium.
Very high amount of dietary fibre.

Maple-Cornmeal Muffins

These cornmeal muffins get a big taste attitude from soy and maple syrup.

2 cups	all-purpose flour	500 mL
¼ cup	granulated sugar	50 mL
1 cup	cornmeal	250 mL
3 tsp	baking powder	15 mL
½ tsp	baking soda	2 mL
½ tsp	salt	2 mL
1	egg, lightly beaten	1
1½ cups	unsweetened soy beverage	375 mL
¼ cup	maple syrup	50 mL
¼ cup	melted butter or vegetable oil	50 mL

1. Preheat oven to 375°F (190°C). Grease 12 muffin cups or coat with cooking spray. In a large bowl, using a fork, stir flour with sugar, cornmeal, baking powder, baking soda and salt until well blended. Make a well in centre. Then whisk egg with soy beverage and maple syrup. Stir into flour mixture with butter just until mixed. Spoon into muffin cups. Bake in centre of preheated oven until a cake tester inserted into middle of muffin comes out clean, from 23 to 25 minutes. Serve warm. Cooked muffins will keep well at room temperature for 2 days or can be frozen.

MAKES: 12 large muffins

PREPARATION TIME: 10 minutes / BAKING TIME: 23 minutes

Nutrients per muffin: 4.5 g protein, 5.2 g total fat (2.6 g saturated, 28 mg cholesterol), 34.1 g carbohydrates, 1.3 mg iron, 41 mg calcium, 258 mg sodium, 1.2 g fibre, 201 calories

vitamin C

lycopene

beta carotene

Tomatoes

Tomatoes burst with lycopene, a red pigment
that is one of our most powerful antioxidants.
Some studies have shown that women with
high levels of lycopene in their blood were less
likely to develop precancerous signs of cervical
cancer. Another study found that men who ate
10 servings a week of cooked tomatoes had
the lowest risk of prostate cancer. This
phytochemical benefit comes from fresh
and canned tomatoes, purées and sauces.

antioxidants

Grilled Stuffed Plum Tomatoes

Oval-shaped plum tomatoes are fleshier and more flavourful than regular ones, but also contain vitamins C and A as well as potassium and fibre. Filled with herbed feta and fresh mint, these warm tomatoes are fantastic as a side dish, appetizer or vegetarian main course.

7	large plum tomatoes	7
1 tsp	olive oil	5 mL
1 cup	crumbled feta	250 mL
2 tbsp	finely chopped fresh mint or basil or basil pesto	30 mL
¼ tsp	freshly ground black pepper	1 mL

1. Lightly grease grill and preheat barbecue to high. Halve tomatoes lengthwise. Gently squeeze out juice and seeds. Using a knife, cut out centre pulp from halves, forming tomato shells. Finely chop pulp and place in a bowl. Finely chop 2 tomato halves, then add to bowl. Brush remaining tomato halves all over with oil. Place on grill, cut-side down, over high heat. Barbecue, without turning, until marked on cut side, about 5 minutes.

2. Meanwhile, stir feta, mint and pepper into tomatoes in bowl. After 5 minutes of grilling, remove tomato halves. Spoon tomato-cheese mixture into hollow of each grilled tomato half, pressing filling gently. Place tomatoes back on grill, filling-side up. Cover and grill until tomatoes are hot, from 4 to 5 minutes. Alternatively, cook tomatoes, bottom-side up, on a greased baking sheet in a 450°F (230°C) oven for 5 minutes. Turn, add cheese mixture, then broil until cheese is tinged with brown, about 1 minute.

MAKES: 6 side-dish servings
PREPARATION TIME: 10 minutes / GRILLING TIME: 9 minutes

Nutrients per serving: 3.7 g protein, 5.3 g total fat (3.2 g saturated, 18 mg cholesterol), 4.6 g carbohydrates, 0.6 mg iron, 110 mg calcium, 238 mg sodium, 1.1 g fibre, 78 calories

Good source of vitamin B12.

Summertime Fried Tomatoes on Toast

When tomatoes are plentiful, this spiced dish, served with poached or fried eggs and crispy bacon or sausages, makes the quintessential cottage breakfast.

¼ tsp	each of ground cumin, cinnamon, salt and granulated sugar	1 mL
2	medium-size ripe but firm tomatoes	2
1 tbsp	olive oil	15 mL
2	minced garlic cloves	2
2	thick slices bread	2
	freshly ground black pepper	

1. In a small bowl, stir cumin with cinnamon, salt and sugar. Set aside. Using a paring knife, cut stem end out of tomatoes and discard. Slice tomatoes into ½-inch (1-cm) rounds.

2. Heat oil in a wide frying pan over medium heat. Add garlic and sauté, stirring often, for 2 minutes. Then increase heat to medium-high. Add tomatoes and sprinkle with seasoning mixture. Fry until bottoms are slightly browned, about 3 minutes. Using a wide metal spatula, turn and cook until both sides are lightly browned, about 2 minutes.

3. Meanwhile, toast bread. Place toast on plates and arrange tomatoes over top. Drizzle with any pan juices. Grind pepper over top.

MAKES: 2 servings

PREPARATION TIME: 10 minutes / COOKING TIME: 7 minutes

Nutrients per serving: 4.6 g protein, 8.5 g total fat (1.3 g saturated, 0 mg cholesterol), 26.8 g carbohydrates, 2.2 mg iron, 63 mg calcium, 511 mg sodium, 2.6 g fibre, 197 calories

Good source of vitamin C and folic acid.
Moderate amount of dietary fibre.

Great Fiery Gazpacho

Everyone loves gazpacho! Enjoy this chilled no-cook soup — it's one of our most requested recipes. If you don't want the kick, omit the jalapeños.

6	large very ripe tomatoes	6
½	English cucumber, peeled	½
1	sweet red pepper, seeded	1
1 to 2	jalapeño peppers, seeded	1 to 2
½ cup	coarsely chopped sweet onion	125 mL
1 tbsp	olive oil	15 mL
2 tbsp	red or white wine vinegar	30 mL
1	minced garlic clove	1
½ tsp	each of salt, celery salt and dried leaf oregano	2 mL
¼ tsp	each of hot pepper sauce and Worcestershire sauce	1 mL
4	large fresh basil leaves or ½ tsp (1 mL) dried basil	4

1. Cut tomatoes and cucumber into chunks. Coarsely chop peppers. Place in a food processor with remaining ingredients. Whirl until vegetables are finely chopped. Refrigerate for at least 2 hours before serving.

MAKES: 5 cups (1.25 L)

PREPARATION TIME: 20 minutes / REFRIGERATION TIME: 2 hours

Nutrients per ½ cup (125 mL): 1.3 g protein, 1.8 g total fat (0.2 g saturated, 0 mg cholesterol), 7.1 g carbohydrates, 0.7 mg iron, 14 mg calcium, 186 mg sodium, 1.7 g fibre, 44 calories

Excellent source of vitamin C.
Good source of vitamin A.

Savory All-Purpose Tomato Sauce

Thyme, oregano and basil lend a robust edge to this thick 'n' rich, slow-simmered multi-purpose sauce. It makes about 10 cups (2.5 L) that can be frozen. Fabulous over pasta, fish or scrambled eggs.

6 lbs	tomatoes, preferably plum, about 32	3 kg
2 tbsp	olive oil	30 mL
2	medium-size onions, chopped	2
6	minced garlic cloves	6
1	large celery stalk, coarsely chopped	1
1½ tsp	each of dried leaf thyme and leaf oregano	7 mL
¾ tsp	salt	3 mL
¾ tsp	freshly ground black pepper	3 mL
1	bay leaf	1
1½ tsp	granulated sugar (optional)	7 mL
½ cup	chopped fresh basil	125 mL

1. Peel tomatoes by slicing a cross in skin on bottom of each. Place about a quarter of them in a bowl and pour boiling water over top. Leave for 10 to 30 seconds until skins split a bit. Drain, then rinse under very cold water. Slip off skins or peel using a sharp knife. Cut away and discard tomato core. Repeat with remaining tomatoes. Then coarsely chop.

2. Heat olive oil in a very large saucepan over medium heat. Add onions, garlic and celery. Stir often until onions are softened, about 5 minutes. Stir in tomatoes, including any juice, thyme, oregano, salt, pepper and bay leaf. Bring to a boil. Then reduce heat to medium-low and simmer, uncovered and stirring occasionally, until thick, about 40 minutes. (If juice and seeds were added, simmer sauce longer to thicken it.)

3. Taste and add sugar if sauce tastes too acidic. Stir in basil and cook for 1 minute. Remove bay leaf and discard. If you prefer a smooth sauce, purée mixture in a food processor or blender, working in batches until smooth. Ladle into containers and seal tightly. Sauce will keep well, covered and refrigerated, for up to 1 week or in the freezer for 3 months.

MAKES: 9½ cups (2.375 L) sauce; use 2 cups (500 mL) to coat ½ lb (250 g) pasta

PREPARATION TIME: 40 minutes / COOKING TIME: 45 minutes

Nutrients per cup (250 mL) sauce: 2.9 g protein, 3.5 g total fat (0.5 g saturated, 0 mg cholesterol), 15.4 g carbohydrates, 1.6 mg iron, 37 mg calcium, 208 mg sodium, 3.9 g fibre, 92 calories

Excellent source of vitamins A and C.
Moderate amount of dietary fibre.

Arrabbiata Tomato Sauce

This classic smooth Italian sauce is not too spicy but full of flavour. It is just as delicious — and a little more rustic — when not puréed. It's made with fresh tomatoes and canned tomato sauce, which are both great sources of lycopene.

¼ cup	olive oil	50 mL
4	large onions, coarsely chopped	4
¼ cup	packed parsley, coarsely chopped	50 mL
4	minced garlic cloves	4
12	regular or 24 plum tomatoes, about 4 lbs (2 kg)	12
14-oz	can tomato sauce	398-mL
2 tsp	dried basil	10 mL
1 tsp	dried leaf oregano	5 mL
1 tsp	hot red chili flakes	5 mL
½ tsp	salt	2 mL
1 tsp	granulated sugar (optional)	5 mL

1. Heat oil in a large saucepan over medium-low heat. Stir in onions, parsley and garlic. Cook, stirring often, until onions are softened, about 15 minutes.

2. Meanwhile, peel tomatoes by slicing a cross in skin on bottom of each. Place in a bowl and pour boiling water over tomatoes. Leave for 10 to 30 seconds until skins split a bit. Drain, then rinse under very cold water. Slip off skins or peel using a sharp knife. Cut away and discard tomato core. Do not seed. Coarsely chop tomatoes. Add tomatoes, including seeds and juice, to onions. Stir in tomato sauce, basil, oregano, chili flakes and salt. Bring to a boil, then reduce heat and boil gently, uncovered and stirring occasionally, until as thick as you like, about 1½ hours. Stir frequently when it thickens near end of cooking. Taste and add sugar, if you find sauce too acidic.

3. For a smooth sauce, purée in a blender, working in batches. Serve over spaghetti, fusilli or penne pasta. Sauce will keep well, covered and refrigerated, for up to 1 week or in the freezer for months. If freezing, ladle sauce into clean, dry containers, leaving a ½-inch (1-cm) headspace, and seal tightly. Or place in heavy resealable plastic bags.

MAKES: 8 cups (2 L); use 1 to 2 cups (250 to 500 mL) to coat ½ lb (250 g) pasta

PREPARATION TIME: 30 minutes / COOKING TIME: 1½ hours

Nutrients per cup (250 mL) sauce: 3.4 g protein, 7.4 g total fat (1 g saturated, 0 mg cholesterol), 18.4 g carbohydrates, 1.8 mg iron, 43 mg calcium, 473 mg sodium, 4.3 g fibre, 139 calories

Excellent source of vitamins A and C.
High amount of dietary fibre.

Freezer Salsa

Here's a big-batch salsa that's better than most store-bought versions. Measure a cup or two into resealable plastic bags, gently press flat, then freeze for easy and swift defrosting whenever a snack attack occurs.

10 to 12	very large ripe tomatoes	10 to 12
1 tbsp	vegetable oil	15 mL
2	large cooking onions or 2 medium Spanish onions	2
8	minced garlic cloves	8
8	jalapeño peppers or 4½-oz (127-g) can diced green chilies	8
2 to 3	sweet green peppers	2 to 3
2	(5½-oz/312-mL) cans tomato paste	2
¼ cup	white or cider vinegar or lime juice	50 mL
1 tbsp	paprika	15 mL
2 tsp	granulated sugar	10 mL
1½ tsp	salt	7 mL
½ tsp	cayenne pepper (optional)	2 mL

1. Core, seed and coarsely chop tomatoes. You should have 10 cups (2.5 L). Peel and finely chop onions.

2. Heat oil in a large wide saucepan over medium heat. When hot, add onions and garlic. Cook, stirring often, until onions have softened, from 7 to 10 minutes. Meanwhile, seed, then very finely chop jalapeños. Seed and coarsely chop sweet peppers.

3. When onions are softened, stir in tomato paste. Then add tomatoes, peppers, vinegar, paprika, sugar and salt. If using canned diced green chilies, stir in contents of can without draining. For an extra hot 'n' spicy hit, stir in cayenne. Bring to a boil, stirring often. Adjust heat, so mixture gently bubbles, and cook, uncovered and stirring occasionally, until thickened, about 30 minutes. Store covered salsa in the refrigerator for up to 1 week or freeze. Flavour improves with overnight refrigeration.

MAKES: 10 cups (2.5 L)

PREPARATION TIME: 45 minutes / COOKING TIME: 40 minutes

Nutrients per tablespoon (15 mL): 0.3 g protein, 0.1 g total fat (0 g saturated, 0 mg cholesterol), 1.6 g carbohydrates, 0.2 mg iron, 3 mg calcium, 24 mg sodium, 0.3 g fibre, 8 calories

Old-Fashioned Chili Sauce

Here's a great rainy day cocooning project from Carol DeGeer of Scarborough, Ontario. Make up a big batch from bargain-priced tomatoes, simmer it for hours and fill your home with some lovely aromas.

12 to 15	large ripe tomatoes	12 to 15
2	large onions	2
3	celery stalks	3
¾ cup	granulated sugar	175 mL
⅔ cup	white vinegar	150 mL
½ tsp	cinnamon	2 mL
½ tsp	ground cloves	2 mL
¼ tsp	salt	1 mL

1. Sterilize enough canning jars and two-piece lids to hold 8 cups (2 L) of sauce. Fill a wide saucepan with water. Bring to a boil over high heat. Dip a few tomatoes in boiling water until skins loosen, from 30 to 60 seconds. Immediately transfer to cold water. Peel and coarsely chop. Repeat with remaining tomatoes. Place 12 cups (3 L) in a large saucepan. Coarsely chop onions and celery and add along with remaining ingredients.

2. Bring tomato mixture to a boil, uncovered and stirring occasionally, over medium-high heat. Reduce heat to low or medium-low to keep sauce gently bubbling. Cook, uncovered and stirring occasionally until thickened, from 2½ to 3 hours. Stir often near end of cooking.

3. Pour into sterilized jars, leaving a ¼-inch (0.5-cm) headspace. Seal as soon as they are filled, using sterilized 2-piece lids. Sauce will thicken as it cools. Once cooled, store in the refrigerator and sauce will keep well for several months. Wonderful on burgers, steaks and scrambled eggs.

MAKES: 8 cups (2 L)

PREPARATION TIME: 30 minutes / COOKING TIME: 2½ hours

Nutrients per tablespoon (15 mL): 0.2 g protein, 0.1 g total fat (0 g saturated, 0 mg cholesterol), 2.4 g carbohydrates, 0.1 mg iron, 2 mg calcium, 7 mg sodium, 0.3 g fibre, 10 calories

Health Wonders

Trumpeting Tomatoes

Oval-shaped plum tomatoes, which are fleshier and more flavourful than regular slicing varieties, contain, like all tomatoes, vitamins C and A and potassium and fibre. Cooked and canned tomatoes are also one of the best sources of lycopene, a red pigment which is believed to have antioxidant properties. You might want to pass on canned tomato juice, which is often high in added salt.

Although fresh tomatoes are filled with lycopene, it's the cooked or canned ones that are easier for your body to use.

How Much to Eat?

Research is not clear as to how many servings of lycopene-rich foods to eat each week for maximum health benefits. Some suggestions aim for 7 to 10 servings, although a few servings a week should do it.

A serving includes ½ cup (125 mL) of tomato or spaghetti sauce, one medium tomato or a slice of pizza with tomato sauce (you might want to go light on the cheese, though).

A Cut Above

Most people slice tomatoes horizontally, but if sliced vertically – from stem end to bottom – they'll retain more juice. To freeze, cut stem ends from ripe unpeeled tomatoes, then freeze tomatoes. Frozen tomatoes can be held under hot running water and skins will slip off. Use in soups, stews and sauces.

Tomatoes and Heart Disease

Next time you order pizza, ask for a double helping of tomatoes. Eating tomatoes, especially cooked ones, can help reduce the risk of cardiovascular disease. Lycopene, which gives tomatoes a bright red colour, also prevents the buildup of fatty plaque on artery walls by gobbling up free radicals, unstable oxygen molecules (see page 4).

Chunky Vegetable Lentil Soup

This quick-to-prepare low-fat soup from The Canadian Dietitian Association's Cookbook, Great Food Fast (Robert Rose), comes from Lynn Roblin, a registered dietitian in Oakville, Ontario. Send it to school in a thermos with teenage vegetarians or pack it to take to the office.

2 cups	water	500 mL
1	vegetable bouillon cube	1
1	large carrot, chopped, about 1 cup (250 mL)	1
28-oz	can diced tomatoes, including juice	796-mL
19-oz	can lentils, drained and rinsed	540-mL
2	minced garlic cloves	2
1 tsp	dried basil	5 mL
½ tsp	dried thyme	2 mL
½ tsp	ground cumin	2 mL

1. In a large saucepan, bring water to a boil. Add bouillon and stir until dissolved. Add carrot. Cover and cook over medium heat for 10 minutes. Add tomatoes along with juice, lentils, garlic, basil, thyme and cumin. Cover and bring to a boil. Uncover, reduce heat and simmer over medium heat, stirring frequently, until carrots are tender, about 10 minutes. Serve right away or cover and refrigerate. Soup will keep well for at least 3 days. Good with cheddar cheese and whole grain toast.

MAKES: 6 cups (1.5 L)

PREPARATION TIME: 5 minutes / COOKING: 20 minutes

Nutrients per cup (250 mL): 7.6 g protein, 0.8 g total fat (0.1 g saturated, 0 mg cholesterol), 21.6 g carbohydrates, 3.4 mg iron, 61 mg calcium, 494 mg sodium, 4.7 g fibre, 116 calories

Excellent source of vitamin A and folic acid.
Good source of vitamin B6.
High amount of dietary fibre.

Saffron Tomato Shrimp Sauce

A pinch of saffron crowns the flavours in this saucy pasta toss that's ready in minutes. Don't shy away from this recipe because of the shrimp, which have been given a bad rap nutritionally. Yes, shrimp do have more cholesterol that most other shellfish, but they are very low in saturated fat, which is more likely to raise your blood cholesterol levels than the cholesterol.

4	round or 8 plum tomatoes	4
1 tbsp	butter or olive oil	15 mL
¼ cup	finely chopped shallots or 1 tbsp (15 mL) minced garlic	50 mL
½ cup	white wine	125 mL
½ tsp	granulated sugar	2 mL
¼ tsp	salt	1 mL
⅛ tsp	saffron threads	0.5 mL
pinch	cayenne pepper	pinch
1 lb	shelled shrimp or bay scallops	500 g
3	green onions, finely sliced	3

1. Coarsely chop tomatoes. You should have about 4 cups (1 L). Melt butter in a large wide frying pan over medium-high heat. Add shallots. Cook, stirring often, about 1 minute. Add tomatoes, wine, sugar and seasonings.

2. Bring to a boil, then adjust heat so mixture gently boils. Cook, uncovered and stirring often, until mixture is reduced in volume and thickened, about 7 minutes. Stir in shrimp. Do not thaw if frozen. Cook until pink and hot, about 3 minutes for precooked and 5 minutes for raw shrimp. Stir in green onions. Toss with pasta or spoon over rice.

MAKES: 4 servings
PREPARATION TIME: 15 minutes / COOKING TIME: 15 minutes

Nutrients per serving: 25.5 g protein, 5.3 g total fat (2.2 g saturated, 180 mg cholesterol), 13.9 g carbohydrates, 3.5 mg iron, 56 mg calcium, 363 mg sodium, 3.4 g fibre, 211 calories

Excellent source of vitamins A, B12 and C.
Moderate amount of dietary fibre.

Roasted Tomato Pepper Soup

This roasted vegetable soup is delicious with just a dollop of light sour cream. Serve it either piping hot or chilled.

16	plum or 8 round tomatoes	16
2	large sweet red peppers	2
1	onion	1
2	large garlic cloves, peeled	2
1 tbsp	olive oil	15 mL
2 cups	chicken broth	500 mL
1 tsp	finely chopped fresh thyme or ½ tsp (2 mL) dried leaf thyme	5 mL
¼ tsp	each of salt and freshly ground black pepper	1 mL
pinch	granulated sugar (optional)	pinch
½ cup	light sour cream (optional)	125 mL

1. Place oven rack at highest level. Preheat oven to 450°F (230°C). Lightly oil a large baking sheet with shallow sides, such as a jelly roll pan. Cut tomatoes in half, lengthwise if plum or crosswise if round, then seed by holding over the sink and squeezing out all seeds and juice. Seed and quarter peppers. Peel and cut onion in half. Place tomatoes cut-side down and peppers cut-side up in a single layer on an oiled baking sheet. Place onion in corners of pan and whole garlic cloves in centre of pan. Drizzle with oil.

2. Bake, uncovered and without turning, on highest rack of 450°F (230°C) oven until vegetables are very soft and edges are browned, about 25 minutes. Remove from oven. When cool enough to handle, discard any tomato and pepper skin that will easily pull away. In a food processor, whirl vegetables until puréed. Add chicken broth and thyme, salt and pepper. Whirl until mixed. Taste and add more salt and pinches of sugar, if needed. When ready to serve, heat until piping hot or refrigerate and serve cold. Top each serving with a dollop of sour cream, if you want. Covered and refrigerated, soup will keep well for 3 days or it can be frozen.

MAKES: 4 cups (1 L)

PREPARATION TIME: 20 minutes / BAKING TIME: 25 minutes

Nutrients per cup (250 mL): 5.7 g protein, 4.8 g total fat (0.8 g saturated, 0 mg cholesterol), 18.7 g carbohydrates, 2 mg iron, 38 mg calcium, 553 mg sodium, 4.5 g fibre, 128 calories

Excellent source of vitamins A and C. **Good source of** vitamin B6 and folic acid.
High amount of dietary fibre.

Spiced Tomatoes and Olives

These colourful nibbles are perfect to serve with cocktails by the pool, on the patio or dock. Although the lycopene in tomatoes is most easily absorbed by the body when heated, this nutritious appetizer is much healthier than taco chips. And you still get vitamin C and beta carotene from the tomatoes.

2 cups	red and yellow teardrop or grape-size tomatoes or cherry tomatoes	500 mL
1 cup	kalamata or mixed olives	250 mL
1	lemon	1
2 tbsp	olive oil	30 mL
2	minced garlic cloves	2
½ tsp	hot red chili flakes	2 mL
1	sprig rosemary or 2 sprigs thyme, snipped into pieces about 1 inch (2.5 cm) long	1
1 tbsp	finely chopped fresh oregano or 1 tsp (5 mL) dried oregano	15 mL

1. Remove and discard tomato stems. Wash tomatoes and pat dry. Place in a medium-size bowl. Add olives. Using a citrus zester or vegetable peeler, remove lemon peel in long thin strips. If using a vegetable peeler, thinly slice peel. Add peel to tomatoes.

2. Place oil in a small measuring cup or bowl. Stir in garlic, chili flakes, rosemary and oregano. Pour over tomato mixture and toss to combine. Mixture is best marinated at room temperature, stirring occasionally, from 3 to 4 hours before serving. Or cover and refrigerate overnight, stirring occasionally. It will keep for several days in the refrigerator.

MAKES: 3 cups (750 mL)

PREPARATION TIME: 10 minutes / MARINATING TIME: 3 hours

Nutrients per ¼ cup (50 mL): 0.5 g protein, 6.4 g total fat (0.8 g saturated, 0 mg cholesterol), 2.3 g carbohydrates, 0.3 mg iron, 14 mg calcium, 372 mg sodium, 0.8 g fibre, 64 calories

complex

carbohydrates

Whole grains

We should be eating three servings a day, but we're averaging just one. Even this single serving, however, may cut our risk of suffering from heart disease. Whole grain fibre could also reduce our risk of diabetes, colon cancer and high blood pressure. Look for whole grain breads, cereals, brown rice and quinoa.

Cumin and Carrot Bulgur Salad

Add a little cool fibre to your patio dinners. You'll also get beta carotene from the carrots and iron from the raisins. Serve this Middle Eastern toss with a selection of cheeses such as feta or goat, warm flat bread and a platter of fresh fruits.

1	large carrot or 6 dried apricots	1
1 cup	coarse or medium bulgur	250 mL
2 tbsp	homemade or bottled vinaigrette salad dressing	30 mL
½ tsp	ground cumin	2 mL
¼ to ½ cup	raisins or ½ cup toasted sliced almonds	50 to 125 mL

1. Thinly slice carrot and place in a large bowl. Add bulgur and cover generously with boiling water, about 4 cups (1 L). If using apricots, coarsely chop, but do not add to bulgur. Let stand until bulgur is tender, about 15 minutes for medium or up to 25 minutes for coarse bulgur. Then drain well.

2. Whisk vinaigrette with cumin. Stir into drained bulgur with raisins, almonds and apricots, if using. Serve at room temperature. Refrigerated salad will keep well for 2 days. Do not freeze.

MAKES: 3 cups (750 mL)
PREPARATION TIME: 10 minutes / SOAKING TIME: 15 minutes

Nutrients per ¾ cup (175 mL): 5.1 g protein, 4.4 g total fat (0.8 g saturated, 0 mg cholesterol), 37.6 g carbohydrates, 1.9 mg iron, 29 mg calcium, 24 mg sodium, 5.1 g fibre, 196 calories

Excellent source of vitamin A.
High amount of dietary fibre.

Wild Rice Salad with Grapes

Wild rice, which isn't a rice at all, but a grass seed, is paired here with grapes and ginger for a refreshing party salad that can be made a day ahead. Wild rice has more protein and less calories than white rice (70 calories per half cup (125 mL) cooked compared with 110 for white rice).

¾ cup	uncooked wild rice	175 mL
1 tsp	salt	5 mL
1½ cups	uncooked long-grain rice	375 mL
6	green onions	6
2 cups	halved seedless green grapes	500 mL
¼ cup	olive oil	50 mL
2 tbsp	toasted sesame oil	30 mL
3 tbsp	freshly squeezed lemon or lime juice	45 mL
1 tsp	Dijon mustard	5 mL
2 tsp	liquid honey	10 mL
¼ cup	minced fresh ginger	50 mL
½ cup	finely chopped fresh mint or basil	125 mL

1. In a large wide saucepan, combine wild rice with 5 cups (1.25 L) water and salt. Cover and bring to a boil. Reduce heat to low and simmer, covered, for 40 minutes. Then stir in long-grain rice. Cover and continue simmering until tender, from 20 to 25 more minutes. Turn into a large bowl.

2. Thinly slice onions on a diagonal. Stir into rice along with grapes. In a small bowl, whisk oils with lemon juice, Dijon and honey. Add ginger. Stir into rice mixture to evenly coat. Cover and set aside for at least 1 hour or up to 3 hours and serve at room temperature. Or refrigerate up to 1 day and serve cold. Add mint just before serving because it darkens quickly. Serve scattered with additional mint leaves.

MAKES: 8 cups (2 L)

PREPARATION TIME: 15 minutes / COOKING TIME: 1 hour / STANDING TIME: 1 hour

Nutrients per cup (250 mL): 5.5 g protein, 10.9 g total fat (1.6 g saturated, 0 mg cholesterol), 49.5 g carbohydrates, 34 mg calcium, 303 mg sodium, 2.3 g fibre, 313 calories

Good source of magnesium.
Moderate amount of dietary fibre.

Quinoa Tabbouleh Salad

Nutritious quinoa delivers a load of protein, vitamins and fibre and comes packed with enough amino acids to be labelled a complete protein.

1¾ cups	water	450 mL
1 cup	quinoa	250 mL
½ cup	olive oil	125 mL
¼ cup	freshly squeezed lemon juice	50 mL
½ tsp	salt	2 mL
¼ tsp	chili powder	1 mL
¼	English cucumber	50 mL
2	tomatoes	2
1	green pepper	1
5	green onions	5
1	large bunch parsley	1

1. Pour water into a small saucepan and bring to a boil. Meanwhile, rinse quinoa with cold water several times. Drain and stir into boiling water with a pinch of salt. Reduce heat and simmer, covered, until all water is absorbed and quinoa grains are transparent, from 10 to 15 minutes.

2. In a bowl, whisk oil with lemon juice, salt and chili powder. Pour hot quinoa into oil mixture and toss well. Refrigerate to cool a little.

3. Meanwhile, dice cucumber, tomatoes and green pepper. Thinly slice green onions and finely chop parsley. Stir into cooled quinoa mixture.

MAKES: 8 cups (2 L)

PREPARATION TIME: 15 minutes

Nutrients per cup (250 mL): 3.6 g protein, 8.2 g total fat (1.1 g saturated, 0 mg cholesterol), 19.3 g carbohydrates, 2.9 mg iron, 36 mg calcium, 158 mg sodium, 2.5 g fibre, 159 calories

Excellent source of vitamin C.
Good source of folic acid.
Moderate amount of dietary fibre.

Apple Wheat Berry Salad

Whole wheat kernels or wheat berries are a delicious way to eat your grains. These pure whole wheat kernels require a longer cooking time, but you'll find their crunchy, nut-flavored taste worth it. Cook up a big batch to have in the refrigerator ready for everything from breakfast cereal to salads. Wheat berries are readily available in health food stores. Some people suggest rinsing the berries before cooking, but we don't find that necessary.

½ cup	whole wheat kernels or wheat berries	125 mL
1	red pepper, cored, seeded and chopped	1
3	green onions, thinly sliced	3
1	apple, peeled and chopped	1
½ cup	toasted almonds, chopped	125 mL
1 tbsp	balsamic vinegar	15 mL
¼ tsp	Dijon mustard	1 mL
pinch	each of salt and freshly ground black pepper	pinch
2 to 3 tbsp	olive oil	30 to 45 mL

1. In a large saucepan, bring 4 cups (1 L) water to a boil. Add wheat berries and simmer, covered, until wheat berries are tender but still chewy, from 1 to 1½ hours. Drain well. Place in a medium-size bowl. Add red pepper, green onions, apple and nuts.

2. Whisk vinegar with Dijon, salt and pepper. Then whisk in olive oil. Toss with wheat berry mixture. Salad can be enjoyed right away or refrigerated until chilled. Once cold, stir well and cover. It will keep well for several days.

MAKES: 4 servings
PREPARATION TIME: 10 minutes / COOKING TIME: 1 hour

Nutrients per serving: 5.9 g protein, 15.5 g total fat (1.8 g saturated, 0 mg cholesterol), 27 g carbohydrates, 1.6 mg iron, 61 mg calcium, 16 mg sodium, 5.1 g fibre, 255 calories

Excellent source of vitamin C and magnesium.
Good source of vitamin A.
High amount of dietary fibre.

Chocolate-Banana Muffins

Yes, it is possible to have your chocolate and whole grains, too. And the bananas add potassium, natural sweetness and moistness, reducing the need for oil. Amazingly enough, each bite comes with ingredients from the four essential food groups.

1	egg	1
¼ cup	vegetable oil	50 mL
1 cup	buttermilk	250 mL
1½ tsp	vanilla	7 mL
½ cup	brown sugar	125 mL
1 cup	mashed banana, about 2 ripe bananas	250 mL
1 cup	all-purpose flour	250 mL
1 cup	whole wheat flour	250 mL
¾ cup	natural bran	175 mL
¼ cup	cocoa powder	50 mL
1 tsp	baking powder	5 mL
1 tsp	baking soda	5 mL
¾ tsp	salt	4 mL
½ cup	coarsely chopped nuts (optional)	125 mL
¼ cup	chocolate chips (optional)	50 mL

1. Preheat oven to 425°F (220°C). Grease 12 muffin cups or line with paper cups. In a medium-size bowl, whisk egg with oil and buttermilk, then vanilla. Stir in sugar until dissolved, then banana.

2. In a large bowl, using a fork, stir flours with bran, cocoa, baking powder and soda, salt and nuts, if using. Make a well in the centre of dry ingredients. Pour banana mixture into well and stir just until blended. Do not overmix. Stir in chocolate chips, if using.

3. Spoon mixture into muffin cups. Bake in centre of preheated oven until a tester inserted into a muffin comes out clean, about 14 minutes.

MAKES: 12 muffins

PREPARATION TIME: 15 minutes / BAKING TIME: 14 minutes

Nutrients per muffin without nuts or chocolate chips: 4.7 g protein, 5.9 g total fat (0.8 g saturated, 19 mg cholesterol), 33.1 g carbohydrates, 1.8 mg iron, 54 mg calcium, 293 mg sodium, 4.1 g fibre, 191 calories

Good source of magnesium.
High amount of dietary fibre.

Health Wonders

Fibre and Weight Loss

Forget about counting fat grams. Filling up on fibre will help keep your waistline in check. A study of 3,000 people ages 18 to 30 published in the *Journal of the American Medical Association* reveals those who ate the most fibre — up to 25 grams a day — were the least likely to gain weight, regardless of how much fat they ate. High-fibre diets stave off weight gain by reducing insulin secretions, say researchers. Too much insulin in your blood can increase appetite, slow metabolism and put you at risk for heart disease. Fibre fans have better blood pressure readings and lower levels of insulin, which reduce their risk of cardiovascular disease.

Cereal Goods

Pouring skim or low-fat milk, soy milk or rice milk over your cereal instead of whole milk keeps the nutritional value high without the fat. Other alternatives might include dousing your grains in orange or apple juice. Or add low-fat yogurt or fresh fruit to your bowl for a quick nutritious breakfast or midnight snack. For more cereal options, see page 143.

Cinnamon-Oatmeal Muffins

Here's a substantial muffin with great looks, texture and taste. As well as the healthy oats, they are packed with four sources of calcium — almonds, milk, molasses and currants.

½ cup	whole almonds, preferably unblanched	125 mL
2 tbsp	brown sugar	30 mL
1	egg	1
1½ cups	milk	625 mL
¼ cup	molasses	50 mL
2 cups	all-purpose flour	500 mL
1 cup	rolled oats, large flake, quick or minute	250 mL
3 tsp	baking powder	15 mL
½ tsp	baking soda	2 mL
1½ tsp	cinnamon	7 mL
¼ tsp	nutmeg	1 mL
½ tsp	salt	2 mL
½ cup	granulated sugar	125 mL
¼ cup	melted butter, cooled	50 mL
1 cup	raisins or currants	250 mL

1. Preheat oven to 375°F (190°C). Coat 12 muffin cups with cooking spray. Chop almonds and mix with brown sugar. In a bowl, whisk egg. Stir in milk and molasses. Measure flour, oats, baking powder, soda, seasonings, then sugar into a large mixing bowl. Stir with a fork until well mixed, then make a well in centre. Pour in egg mixture and then melted butter, stirring until just combined. Stir in raisins.

2. Spoon into muffin cups. Batter will almost fill cups. Evenly sprinkle with almond mixture. Bake in centre of preheated oven until golden and a cake tester inserted into muffin centre comes out clean, from 20 to 25 minutes. Cool in cups 5 minutes. Muffins are wonderful warm. They will keep well at room temperature in a plastic bag for up to 2 days or can be frozen for a month or more. Bonus calcium: Stirring ¼ cup (50 mL) non-fat dried milk into flour mixture adds 200 milligrams of calcium and 6 grams of protein to the recipe.

MAKES: 12 large muffins
PREPARATION TIME: 15 minutes / BAKING TIME: 20 minutes

Nutrients per muffin: 6.4 g protein, 8.6 g total fat (3.3 g saturated, 31 mg cholesterol), 49.8 g carbohydrates, 2.2 mg iron, 118 mg calcium, 275 mg sodium, 2.4 g fibre, 294 calories

Good source of magnesium and iron.
Moderate amount of dietary fibre.

Apple Squares
with Zesty Crumble Coating

This crumbly fresh-fruit version of date squares takes no cooking skill to make. Serve it with warmed frozen yogurt or light sour cream and it's a most satisfying dessert brimming with whole grains and iron.

8	large ripe apples	8
½ cup	granulated sugar	125 mL
2 tsp	cinnamon	5 mL
1 cup	raisins (optional)	250 mL
2½ cups	rolled oats (not instant)	625 mL
2 cups	all-purpose flour	500 mL
1½ cups	brown sugar	375 mL
1 cup	butter, at room temperature	250 mL
	finely grated peel of 2 oranges	

1. Peel and core apples. Slice into ½-inch (1-cm) thick wedges. Combine in a large saucepan with sugar, cinnamon and raisins, if using. Cook over medium heat, uncovered, until apples are fork-tender, about 15 minutes. Stir often.

2. Meanwhile, preheat oven to 350°F (180°C). Place all crumble ingredients in a large bowl. Work with your hands until evenly mixed. Firmly press half the mixture in a 9x13-inch (3-L) ungreased pan. Firmly press down until bottom is evenly covered. Pour hot apple mixture over top and smooth. Evenly spoon remaining crumble mixture over apples.

3. Bake in centre of preheated oven until golden brown, from 30 to 40 minutes. Then place pan on a rack until cooled to room temperature. Cut into squares and serve with vanilla ice cream. Cover leftover squares loosely and refrigerate up to 3 days or freeze.

MAKES: 24 squares
PREPARATION TIME: 30 minutes / COOKING TIME: 15 minutes
BAKING TIME: 30 minutes

Nutrients per square: 2.6 g protein, 8.5 g total fat (4.9 g saturated, 21 mg cholesterol), 41.4 g carbohydrates, 1.2 mg iron, 28 mg calcium, 83 mg sodium, 3.2 fibre, 245 calories

Moderate amount of dietary fibre.

Three-Grain Power Porridge

Stick-to-the-ribs porridge gives you a jump-start on your daily fibre, vitamin, mineral and protein requirements. While most of us think of traditional oatmeal when we think of porridge, grains such as buckwheat kernels (kasha), barley, cracked rye and whole wheat kernels qualify as porridge and offer a tasty and nutritious alternative.

1½ cups	water	375 mL
½ cup	milk, preferably 1%	125 mL
¼ cup	each of rye flakes, barley flakes and rolled oats	50 mL
⅛ tsp	salt	0.5 mL

1. Mix all ingredients together in a heavy-bottomed saucepan. Cover and place over medium heat. When mixture comes to a boil, reduce heat to low and simmer, stirring occasionally, from 15 to 20 minutes. To microwave, reduce water quantity to 1 cup (250 mL). Mix with remaining ingredients in a microwave-safe bowl. Cover and cook on high for 3 minutes. Stir, cover and continue cooking from 4 to 5 minutes, stirring each minute.

2. Stir in any of the following and enjoy: 2 tbsp (30 mL) brown sugar, ¼ tsp (1 mL) vanilla, ⅛ tsp (0.5 mL) cinnamon, a pinch of nutmeg.

MAKES: 2 cups (500 mL)

PREPARATION TIME: 5 minutes / COOKING TIME: 15 minutes

Nutrients per cup: 6.4 g protein, 1.8 g total fat (0.6 g saturated, 2 mg cholesterol), 24.2 g carbohydrates, 1.1 mg iron, 91 mg calcium, 181 mg sodium, 4.3 g fibre, 134 calories

Good source of magnesium.
High amount of dietary fibre.

Health Wonders

Hot Porridge Possibilities

Grain	Cook	Extras
Barley Very mild in flavour and slightly chewy, barley comes whole, ground and flaked. Whole barley is more nutritious because it has more vitamins and fibre than the dehulled pearl barley, which has been stripped of many of its nutrients. It's readily available in health food stores. Although pearl and pot barley are similar, pot barley is bigger.	Simmer 1 part barley to 2 parts water, covered, for 45 minutes.	Cook with rolled oats. Add a pinch each of nutmeg, cinnamon and grated orange peel.
Buckwheat Kernels (Kasha) Whole unpolished kernels (called kasha when roasted). Nutty mild flavour and soft texture.	Simmer 2 parts water to 1 part buckwheat, covered, for 15 minutes.	Cook with rolled oats. Top with yogurt.
Millet Unpolished whole kernels. Bland flavour. Firmer than cream of wheat when cooked.	Simmer 2 parts water to 1 part millet, covered, for 30 minutes.	Top with toasted sesame seeds and hazelnuts.
Oatmeal Ground oat kernels. Sold coarse, medium or fine. Wholesome creamy taste.	If not quick cooking, must simmer 3 parts water to 1 part oatmeal, uncovered, for 25 minutes.	Add raisins and vanilla.
Rolled Oats Steamed and flattened oat kernels. Slightly nutty flavour and soft texture.	Simmer 2 parts water to 1 part oats, covered, for 10 minutes. Quick-cooking rolled oats take $2\frac{1}{2}$ to 5 minutes.	Add raisins or diced dried apricots while cooking.
Steel-cut Oats (Irish or Scottish Oatmeal) Oat kernels cut with a steel blade. Nutty flavour and firm texture.	Simmer 2 parts water to 1 part oats, covered, for at least 30 minutes.	Top with brown sugar and cinnamon.
Whole Wheat Kernels or Wheat Berries Pure whole wheat kernels require a long cooking time. Crunchy, nut-flavoured taste.	Simmer 4 parts water to 1 part wheat berries, covered, for 1 to $1\frac{1}{2}$ hours. Make a big batch to keep in the refrigerator, ready to use.	Serve with skim milk or yogurt topped with raisins, or make a salad (see recipe, page 137).

Picnic Tabbouleh Salad

Our version of this Middle Eastern dish is remarkably low in fat. The large yield makes it perfect for picnics or keeping in the fridge for a couple of days to enjoy whenever you want. It's great for work lunches.

1½ cups	medium or coarse bulgur, about ½ lb (250 g)	375 mL
3 cups	boiling water	750 mL
2	large lemons	2
2 tbsp	olive oil	30 mL
1 tsp	salt	5 mL
¼ tsp	freshly ground black pepper	1 mL
4	minced garlic cloves	4
¼ tsp	cayenne pepper (optional)	1 mL
6	green onions, thinly sliced	6
⅔ to ¾ cup	chopped fresh mint	150 to 175 mL
½ cup	coarsely chopped fresh parsley	125 mL
4	ripe tomatoes	4
	crumbled feta or goat cheese (optional)	

1. Place bulgur in a heatproof bowl. Cover with boiling water. Let stand at room temperature, without stirring, until all water is absorbed and bulgur is just tender, about 45 minutes.

2. Meanwhile, finely grate 1 teaspoon (5 mL) peel from lemons and squeeze ⅓ cup (75 mL) juice into a large bowl. Whisk with oil, salt, black pepper, garlic and cayenne, if using. When bulgur is tender and water is absorbed, stir into dressing until coated. Add onions, ⅔ cup (150 mL) mint and parsley.

3. Slice tomatoes in half and squeeze out juice and seeds. Finely chop pulp. Stir into bulgur. Before serving, taste and add more lemon juice, salt and remaining mint, if needed. Serve immediately or, even better, refrigerate, covered, overnight so flavours blend. Salad will keep in the refrigerator for up to 2 days, but tomatoes will soften. For a nutritionally complete meatless meal, sprinkle with feta or goat cheese.

MAKES: 12 servings

PREPARATION TIME: 20 minutes / STANDING TIME: 45 minutes

Nutrients per serving: 2.9 g protein, 2.6 g total fat (0.4 g saturated, 0 mg cholesterol), 17.3 g carbohydrates, 1.3 mg iron, 26 mg calcium, 202 mg sodium, 3.1 g fibre, 96 calories

Good source of folic acid.
Moderate amount of dietary fibre.

Fruit Crisp with Pecan Topping

This crisp isn't exactly the lowest-fat dessert around, but it is bursting with grains, nuts and fruits including cranberries, often used to treat urinary tract infections.

6 to 8	ripe Bartlett pears, peeled	6 to 8
6	large ripe McIntosh or Spy apples, peeled	6
1 tbsp	freshly squeezed lemon juice	15 mL
1½ cups	fresh or dried cranberries	375 mL
2 tbsp	finely chopped crystallized ginger	30 mL
½ cup	all-purpose flour	125 mL
2 tsp	finely grated lemon or orange peel (optional)	10 mL
½ tsp	each of nutmeg and salt	2 mL
1 tsp	cinnamon	5 mL
⅔ cup	granulated sugar	150 mL
1¼ cups	brown sugar, not packed	300 mL
½ cup	all-purpose flour	125 mL
½ cup	quick-cooking oats	125 mL
1 tsp	cinnamon	5 mL
⅔ cup	cold butter, cut into small cubes	150 mL
1¼ cups	pecan or walnut halves, coarsely chopped	300 mL

1. Preheat oven to 350°F (180°C). Core pears and apples and thinly slice. Place in a large bowl. There should be about 14 cups (3.5 L). Stir in lemon juice. If using fresh cranberries, measure, then slice in half. Stir fresh or dried cranberries into fruit with ginger. Stir flour with peel, spices and granulated sugar. Stir until combined. Sprinkle over fruit and stir to coat. Turn into a buttered 9x13-inch (3-L) baking dish or shallow-sided casserole dish that will hold 12 cups (3 L). Gently press down to even top.

2. Using a fork, stir brown sugar with flour, oats and cinnamon. Add butter. Work between your fingers until clumps are the size of peas. Stir in nuts. Evenly sprinkle over fruit. Do not pat down. Lay a piece of foil loosely over top and bake 15 minutes. Remove foil. Continue baking until fruit is tender, 40 to 50 more minutes. Let stand 5 minutes before serving. Crisp will keep well refrigerated several days.

MAKES: 10 to 12 servings

PREPARATION TIME: 30 minutes / BAKING TIME: 55 minutes

Nutrients per serving: 3.1 g protein, 18.9 g total fat (7.1 g saturated, 28 mg cholesterol), 74.6 g carbohydrates, 2.2 mg iron, 52 mg calcium, 209 mg sodium, 6 g fibre, 459 calories

Good source of iron.
Very high amount of dietary fibre.

Whole Grain Pancake Mix

Whip up a batch for today and store the rest of this wholesome low-fat mix in the refrigerator or freezer, ready for a kid-pleasing supper or big brunch. They taste so much more interesting than plain pancakes.

Whole Grain Pancake Mix

1 cup	rolled oats	250 mL
2 tbsp	each of wheat germ and brown sugar	30 mL
1½ cups	whole wheat flour	375 mL
½ cup	instant skim-milk powder	125 mL
4 tsp	baking powder	20 mL
½ tsp	baking soda	2 mL
¾ tsp	salt	3 mL

For 10 Pancakes

1	egg	1
1 tbsp	vegetable oil	15 mL
½ cup	milk	125 mL
¼ tsp	vanilla	1 mL
¾ cup	Whole Grain Pancake Mix	175 mL

1. For mix, insert metal blade in a food processor. With motor running, pour in oats, wheat germ and sugar. Turn off processor. Add flour, milk powder, baking powder, baking soda and salt. Pulse just until blended. You should have about 2¼ cups (550 mL). Divide into 3 batches of ¾ cup (175 mL) each. Store in sealed plastic bags or tightly sealed glass jars. Mixture must be kept dry. It will keep well in the refrigerator for up to 2 weeks or in the freezer for several months.

2. For 10 small pancakes, beat egg in a large bowl with oil, milk and vanilla. Stir in ¾ cup (175 mL) of Whole Grain Pancake Mix. Let stand for 5 minutes. Meanwhile, heat a large frying pan or griddle over medium heat. Lightly grease hot pan. When drops of water sprinkled on pan bounce, it is hot. Pour scoops of batter onto hot pan. About 2 tablespoons (30 mL) of batter will produce a 3-inch (7.5-cm) wide pancake. Fill pan but don't crowd. Cook until bubbles form on top, about 2 minutes. Turn and cook 2 more minutes. Repeat with remaining batter. Serve with fresh fruit and maple syrup.

MAKES: 10 small pancakes and mix for 20 more

PREPARATION TIME: 10 minutes / STANDING TIME: 5 minutes / COOKING TIME: 4 minutes per pancake

Nutrients per 2 pancakes: 5.6 g protein, 4.8 g total fat (1 g saturated, 46 mg cholesterol), 17.4 g carbohydrates, 1 mg iron, 102 mg calcium, 262 mg sodium, 2.2 g fibre, 132 calories

Moderate amount of dietary fibre.

Herbed Whole Wheat Soda Bread

A good soda bread has a unique slightly tangy taste similar to sour dough but with a lighter texture. This one is made with whole wheat flour, caraway, herbs and buttermilk. It's really terrific and doesn't take eons to make. Great with cheddar and beer for lunch.

1¾ cups	whole wheat flour	425 mL
2 cups	all-purpose flour	500 mL
1 tsp	each of baking soda, salt and dried basil	5 mL
½ tsp	each of dried leaf thyme and leaf oregano	2 mL
1½ tsp	caraway seeds (optional)	7 mL
¼ cup	cold butter	50 mL
1¾ cups	buttermilk or low-fat yogurt	425 mL

1. Set rack just below oven centre so bread will bake in bottom third of oven. This allows bread to bake thoroughly without making top too brown. Preheat oven to 400°F (200°C). In a large bowl, using a fork, stir flours with baking soda, salt, basil, thyme and oregano. Stir in caraway seeds, if using. Using your fingers, rub in butter until mixture is crumbly but tiny pieces of butter can still be seen. Or use a pastry cutter to cut in butter. Pour in buttermilk and stir just until all ingredients are combined.

2. Place dough on a floured surface. With floured hands, shape into a flat round loaf, about 8 inches (20 cm) across. Place loaf on a greased baking sheet and, with a sharp knife, cut a cross into top of load, about ½ inch (1 cm) deep.

3. Bake in preheated oven until a skewer inserted into centre comes out clean and bread is golden brown, from 45 to 55 minutes. Cool about 5 minutes on a wire rack, slice into wedges and serve warm. Bread will keep well for at least 2 days at room temperature and freezes well.

MAKES: 12 slices

PREPARATION TIME: 10 minutes / BAKING TIME: 45 minutes

Nutrients per slice: 5.8 g protein, 4.7 g total fat (2.7 g saturated, 12 mg cholesterol), 30.4 g carbohydrates, 1.6 mg iron, 54 mg calcium, 366 mg sodium, 2.9 g fibre, 184 calories

Moderate amount of dietary fibre.

Chocolate

Women love chocolate – listing it as one of the five pleasures in life, along with shopping, massage, friends and sex. So the question is: Can something that good, be good for you? The answer is yes. Like red wine, chocolate contains antioxidants that may reduce the risk of heart disease. Dark chocolate is the best. It has more nutrients and less sugar. Although you might not think of looking to chocolate for minerals, it also contains iron, calcium, potassium and magnesium, which may help ease the symptoms of PMS, including headaches, mood swings and water retention. But remember, chocolate is still high in fat that will no doubt go directly to your waistline, so let a little go a long way.

Cranberry-Chocolate Cookies

Texture abounds in these chewy cookies rich with cranberries, chocolate and whole grains. One, or okay, maybe two, is all you need to satisfy a chocolate craving. Great with a glass of cold milk.

1½ cups	all-purpose flour	375 mL
½ tsp	baking soda	2 mL
½ tsp	salt	2 mL
¼ tsp	cinnamon	1 mL
5 squares	semisweet chocolate (about 5 oz/140 g)	5 squares
¾ cup	dried cranberries	175 mL
½ cup	toasted walnuts, pecans or almonds	125 mL
¾ cup	unsalted butter, at room temperature	175 mL
½ cup	granulated sugar	125 mL
½ cup	brown sugar	125 mL
1	egg, lightly beaten	1
1 tbsp	freshly squeezed lemon juice	15 mL
1 tsp	vanilla	5 mL
1 cup	rolled oats (not instant)	250 mL

1. Preheat oven to 325°F (160°C). Grease baking sheets. In a small bowl, stir flour with soda, salt and cinnamon until blended. Coarsely chop chocolate and place in another bowl. Mix in cranberries and nuts.

2. In a large bowl, stir butter with a wooden spoon until creamy. Gradually stir in sugars until blended. Stir in egg, lemon juice and vanilla until well combined. Gradually stir in flour mixture and oatmeal until well mixed. Stir in chocolate-nut mixture until evenly distributed.

3. Drop by heaping tablespoonfuls (15 mL), at least 1 inch (2.5 cm) apart, on prepared sheets. Bake in centre of preheated oven until edges are golden and centres seem set when lightly touched, about 12 minutes. Remove from trays and cool on a rack. Store cookies in a sealed container with layers separated by waxed paper. Cookies will keep well at room temperature for 3 days and freeze well.

MAKES: 42 cookies

PREPARATION TIME: 20 minutes / BAKING TIME: 12 minutes

Nutrients per cookie: 1.3 g protein, 5.3 g total fat (2.8 g saturated, 14 mg cholesterol), 13.5 carbohydrates, 0.5 mg iron, 8 mg calcium, 45 mg sodium, 0.8 g fibre, 103 calories

Ultimate Fudge Brownies

These hard-to-resist chewy fudge brownies have a crispy top and toasted pecans for plenty of texture sensation.

5 squares	unsweetened chocolate (about 5 oz/140 g)	5 squares
1 cup	unsalted butter, at room temperature	250 mL
2 cups	granulated sugar	500 mL
4	eggs	4
½ tsp	vanilla	2 mL
½ tsp	salt	2 mL
½ cup	all-purpose flour	125 mL
1 cup	coarsely chopped toasted pecans or walnuts	250 mL

1. Preheat oven to 350°F (180°C). Lightly butter a 9x13-inch (3-L) baking dish or coat with cooking spray. Coarsely chop chocolate. Place in a large saucepan and add butter. Cook over medium-low heat, uncovered and stirring often, especially as mixture begins to melt, until chocolate is mostly melted, about 6 minutes. Remove from heat and stir until smooth.

2. Stir sugar into warm chocolate in saucepan. Then add eggs, one at a time, beating after each addition until blended. Stir in vanilla and salt. Stir in flour just until mixed. Fold in nuts. Spread batter in prepared pan. Bake in centre of preheated oven until top is light brown and crusty and a cake tester inserted in middle comes out almost clean, from 25 to 30 minutes. Brownies are very soft when removed from oven. Cool completely in pan on a rack before cutting. Brownies will keep well, covered, at room temperature, for 3 to 4 days and freeze well.

MAKES: 24 brownies

PREPARATION TIME: 15 minutes

COOKING TIME: 6 minutes / BAKING TIME: 25 minutes

Nutrients per brownie: 2.4 g protein, 15 g total fat (7.2 g saturated, 56 mg cholesterol), 21.2 g carbohydrates, 0.7 mg iron, 13 mg calcium, 60 mg sodium, 1.3 g fibre, 217 calories

Caramel-Pecan Brownies

A crowning layer of citrus-spiked caramel and pecans add glamour to these rich chocolate brownies.

2 squares	unsweetened or bittersweet chocolate, coarsely chopped (about 2 oz/56 g)	2 squares
1 cup	butter	250 mL
⅓ cup	cocoa	75 mL
1½ cups	all-purpose flour	375 mL
1½ cups	granulated sugar	375 mL
½ tsp	salt	1 mL
4	eggs, lightly beaten	4
1½ tsp	vanilla	7 mL
Caramel-Nut Topping		
½ cup	granulated sugar	125 mL
¼ cup	butter	50 mL
¼ cup	orange or cranberry juice concentrate	50 mL
2 tbsp	honey or corn syrup	30 mL
2 cups	pecans, chopped	500 mL

1. Preheat oven to 350°F (180°C). Lightly butter a 9x13-inch (3-L) pan or coat with cooking spray. To make brownies, heat chocolate with butter in a small saucepan over low heat. Stir often until chocolate is melted. Remove from heat and stir in cocoa. In a large mixing bowl, stir flour with sugar and salt. Stir in chocolate mixture. Mix in eggs and vanilla. Spread evenly in prepared pan. Bake in centre of preheated oven for 20 minutes.

2. Meanwhile, to make topping, in a small saucepan, combine sugar, butter, undiluted juice and honey. Bring to a boil over medium heat, then reduce heat and simmer for 3 minutes, stirring almost constantly. Remove from heat.

3. When brownies have baked 20 minutes, sprinkle with pecans, then drizzle with hot syrup. Return to oven. Bake until topping is bubbly, about 20 more minutes. Cool in pan on a rack. Squares will keep well, covered, for up to 2 days and can be frozen.

MAKES: 24 brownies

PREPARATION TIME: 30 minutes / BAKING TIME: 40 minutes / COOKING TIME: 5 minutes

Nutrients per brownie: 3.2 g protein, 18.6 g total fat (7.6 g saturated, 62 mg cholesterol), 28.3 g carbohydrates, 1 mg iron, 16 mg calcium, 157 mg sodium, 1.6 g fibre, 280 calories

Health Wonders

The Bittersweet Truth

For centuries, the world has been enthralled with the taste of chocolate. In North America, every year more than 3 billion pounds is consumed. Whether it's a lick, a sip, a crunch or a melt-in-your-mouth experience, chocolate, we shudder to ourselves, can't be good for us. Well, think again, because everybody's favourite indulgence has some little-known benefits.

Here's the Good News

Chocolate contains a substantial amount of flavonoids. This is the same antioxidant that is available in red wine, green tea and fruits and vegetables and has been receiving a huge amount of press coverage because it's believed to reduce the rate of heart disease. A Harvard study found that men who ate candy and chocolate three or more times a week lived almost a year longer than those who didn't.

The average 1½-ounce (45-gram) chocolate bar contains 10 percent of your daily iron and riboflavin needs. A milk chocolate bar gives you 10 percent of your daily calcium.

The Good and Bad News

The bad news, as we all know, is the high fat content in chocolate. Most of chocolate's flavour comes from cocoa butter. The average chocolate bar gets 50 to 60 percent of its calories from fat. Unsweetened baking chocolate gets 76 percent. The fat in chocolate is the saturated kind, which is not good for a healthy heart. But recent research has shown that cocoa butter, which is a stearic acid, does not elevate blood cholesterol levels like other saturated fats. Stearic acid may in fact cause cholesterol levels to drop without affecting the good cholesterol that helps reduce the risk of heart disease.

Chocolate and Migraines

Although most advice about preventing migraines tells you to avoid chocolate, some researchers are questioning that generally accepted link. Dr. Dawn Marcus of the University of Pittsburgh Medical Center studied 63 women with histories of migraines and tension headaches and found that only three of the women developed headaches after eating chocolate.

Since 50 percent of the women crave chocolate, especially during menstruation or when they are under stress, Dr. Marcus theorizes that the situation in which we crave chocolate may cause the headaches, not the chocolate itself.

Molten Chocolate Cakes

This incredible chocolate hit is from pastry chef Steve Song of Toronto. It's wonderfully rich, but very high in fat. Save it for a party or other special occasion.

2 tbsp	unsweetened cocoa	30 mL
½ cup	unsalted butter	125 mL
8 squares	bittersweet or semisweet chocolate, coarsely chopped (about 8 oz/225 g)	8 squares
8	eggs	8
1 cup	granulated sugar	250 mL
⅔ cup	all-purpose flour	150 mL

1. Lightly butter 12 cups of a muffin tin. Sift cocoa, then use to "flour" buttered cups as you would cake pans. Shake cups to ensure an even coating. Shake out excess over sink. All of cocoa will not be used. Preheat oven to 400°F (200°F). Place butter and chocolate in a bowl. Microwave on medium power, stirring once, until buttered is melted, from 2 to 3 minutes. Stir until smooth. Or melt butter and chocolate in a small saucepan over low heat. Stir often until mixture is smooth, from 4 to 5 minutes.

2. Separate 4 eggs, placing 4 yolks in a large mixing bowl, saving whites for another use. (Whites can be frozen for months.) Add remaining 4 whole eggs and sugar to bowl. Beat with a whisk or electric mixer until lighter in colour, from 3 to 5 minutes. Then while whisking constantly, pour in warm chocolate mixture. When smooth, gradually beat in flour until just combined.

3. Dividing equally, pour batter into prepared muffin cups. Bake in centre of 400°F (200°C) oven until sides are crusty and resemble a muffin, but centres are still soft, about 10 minutes. Do not overbake. Remove from oven. Let stand 5 minutes during which time cake centre will become flattened and appear to fall.

4. Then run a knife around edges. Using a fork to help get underneath, remove each cake from tin and invert onto a dessert plate. Serve hot with a few berries and softly whipped cream.

Make ahead: After letting baked cakes stand 5 minutes, turn out and cool completely on a rack. Wrap and refrigerate up to 2 days or freeze. To reheat, remove wrappings. Thaw if frozen. Place one cold cake bottom-side up on a plate. Microwave, uncovered, on medium power, 30 to 45 seconds or until hot. Or heat, uncovered on a baking sheet, in a preheated 450°F (230°C) oven 4 minutes. Do not overheat.

MAKES: 12 small cakes

PREPARATION TIME: 20 minutes / COOKING TIME: 4 minutes / BAKING TIME: 10 minutes

Nutrients per cake: 5.9 g protein, 21.7 g total fat (12.1 g saturated, 166 mg cholesterol), 27.9 g carbohydrates, 2 mg iron, 34 mg calcium, 28 mg sodium, 3.3 g fibre, 303 calories

Excellent source of magnesium.
Moderate amount of dietary fibre.

Mocha Fondue

Spear pieces of fruit or squares of pound cake into this rich warm chocolate sauce. There's a nice contrast between cool fruit and warm sauce with every bite — and for a nip of brandy or rum, see our Tip, below.

8 squares	semisweet chocolate (about 8 oz/225 g)	8 squares
½ cup	hot espresso or strong coffee	125 mL
3 tbsp	granulated sugar	45 mL
2 tbsp	butter	30 mL
½ tsp	vanilla	2 mL

1. Using a chef's knife, coarsely chop chocolate. Stir coffee with granulated sugar in a small saucepan over low heat until sugar dissolves, about 5 minutes. Add chocolate and butter. Continue cooking, stirring frequently until mixture is smooth, about 3 minutes. Stir in vanilla. Keep warm while serving in a small fondue pot or on a food warming tray set on low.

2. Supply each guest with a long-handled fondue fork for spearing and dipping. Serve with a selection of dippers, such as whole strawberries, chunks of mango, banana and pineapple and cubes of pound cake. For crunch, offer small shortbread and gingerbread cookies.

MAKES: about 1⅓ cups (325 mL), for 6 to 8 servings
PREPARATION TIME: 10 minutes / COOKING TIME: 8 minutes

Microwave method: Dissolve sugar in hot espresso or strong coffee in a 4-cup (1-L) measure. Add chocolate pieces and butter. Microwave, uncovered and stirring twice, on medium-high power until hot and mixture is smooth, from 2 to 4 minutes. Stir in vanilla.

TIP: For an extra jolt of flavour, place 2 tablespoons (30 mL) brandy, rum or Irish cream liqueur into a measuring cup. Add enough hot espresso or strong coffee to bring the level up to ½ cup (125 mL), then use in recipe.

Nutrients per tablespoon (15 mL): 0.5 g protein, 4.3 g total fat (2.6 g saturated, 3 mg cholesterol), 8.5 g carbohydrates, 0.3 mg iron, 4 mg calcium, 12 mg sodium, 0.6 g fibre, 67 calories

Recipe Index by Nutrient

Need more folic acid or calcium in your diet? Let this handy guide help you locate the recipes that are an excellent or particularly good source of the nutrients you need.

Index